The

SCOTTISH

Football Book

No. 16

The
SCOTTISH
Football Book

No. 16

Edited by
HUGH TAYLOR

STANLEY PAUL
London

STANLEY PAUL & CO LTD
178–202 Great Portland Street, London W1

AN IMPRINT OF THE HUTCHINSON GROUP

London Melbourne Sydney
Auckland Johannesburg Cape Town
and agencies throughout the world

First published 1970

*This book has been set in Baskerville, printed in Great Britain
by offset litho at Taylor Garnett Evans & Co Ltd, Watford, Herts,
and bound by William Brendon, at Tiptree, Essex*

ISBN 0 09 103300 4

Contents

The Editor says...

A WARM welcome to this new Scottish Football Book.

What a season it was, the sizzling season of 1969–70. It was sad that, for Celtic, once again the team of the year, the season ended in tragedy, defeat by Feyenoord in the European Cup Final in Milan.

But Celtic will rise again, will win the European Cup, blue riband of our great game ... that's what manager Jock Stein forecasts and who can say he'll be wrong?

And there is no doubt that had Celtic shown the form—their real form!—that trounced Leeds United and so many other teams they must have become the only British club to win the European Cup twice. Anyhow, they proved themselves the top side in Britain—and in Scotland they won their greatest League triumph—a winning margin of 12 points which is a record for the club. Now and again they stumbled; they were chased for spells by Rangers and Hibernian; but, in the end, they were worthy champions.

More important. In winning their fifth title in succession under Jock Stein, Celtic also blended into first team resources a number of youngsters who can keep the flag flying at Parkhead for a long time—youngsters such as David Hay, George Connelly, Lou Macari.

Rangers were again runners-up. But there is new determination at Ibrox. Willie Waddell has taken over as manager from David White and new ideas, introduction of the old Ibrox spirit and a relentless will to win may make Rangers a more formidable team soon.

Sadder glimpses into the Scottish soccer scene, however, are ... the serious lack of challenge to the Old Firm. It was heartening for Edinburgh to see Hibernian and Hearts finish high in the table—but they did not show the power and resiliency to make them all-the-way challengers.

It was sad to see Kilmarnock and Dunfermline, for so long the clubs most likely to challenge the Big Two of Glasgow, so far down—but they will surely come again.

Up come Falkirk and Cowdenbeath to the first division and we welcome them upstairs. Down went Raith Rovers and Partick Thistle—and the downfall of the Jags caused many a tear, for they hadn't been relegated before and they are one of our most popular clubs.

On the bright side, Scotland showed much more skill and spirit in the home internationals, although, once again, we failed in the World Cup. New players are coming up, there is a Celtic-like attitude in our international side—and the future seems brighter than for a long time.

And the great triumph of Aberdeen in the Scottish Cup gives hope that the Dons are breaking through to glory in other competitions as well as the cup.

Let's hope the new season has Scotland starting with a bang in the European Nations Competition—and with all our clubs who face foreign foes in the big European tournaments making a hit.

I hope you enjoy this new Scottish Football Book. I'm sorry I can't talk about all your clubs; we just haven't the space. Thanks for your views. I enjoy hearing from you.

HUGH TAYLOR

Dons back at the top of the class

THE players of Aberdeen were quietly seething. Even the luxurious hotel in which they were staying did little to make them feel happier. So ruffled were their feelings that they had no time to admire the beautiful golf courses, the magnificent scenery and the perfect service of Gleneagles.

You could hardly blame them. For it was the eve of the Scottish Cup Final and Aberdeen were going into it the underdogs of underdogs. Never had there been a Hampden occasion when one team was so contemptuously dismissed. The bookmakers had made it almost a walk-over—and not for Aberdeen. For their opponents, Celtic, who were on the crest of a wave. Celtic were hottest favourites of all time at the incredible odds of three-to-one on. Aberdeen were at six-to-one against.

So Aberdeen were angry young men. It was true Celtic had won the Scottish first division title once again, true they were playing with tremendous skill and pace, true they were on top of the world after beating Leeds United at Elland Road in the first leg of the European Cup semi-final.

Yet not long before Aberdeen had achieved a brilliant victory over Celtic—and at Parkhead. And the Dons were agreed that they would bring old glory back to their northern city, glory that had escaped the famous ground of Pittodrie since Aberdeen won the league championship in 1954–55 and the League Cup the following season.

Manager Eddie Turnbull, former great Hibernian and Scotland player, summed it up grimly. 'We see no reason for any kind of inferiority complex,' he said. 'After all we had four cracking matches with Celtic this season. We lost two, won one, drew the other . . . and in none of the games was there more than a goal in it. I can't understand why we are given no chance. We'll just have to see about that.'

You might have thought there would be

Celtic lose dramatic Final to young Cock's O'the North

a world of difference in the attitude of Celtic, installed hardly 100 miles away from Aberdeen in the equally fashionable Marine Hotel at Troon, on the breezy Ayrshire coast.

Yet although Celtic, the team of seasoned warriors going so professionally for a mass to honours to match the medals on the chest of an American general, were such hot favourites, there was no superiority complex in their thoughts about the final.

They realised it was going to be as tough a match as they had faced all season and, as always, manager Jock Stein had briefed them as thoroughly as though the Celts had been facing Leeds United or AC Milan.

After all, as Stein pointed out, there was a lot of Celtic pride at stake. Celtic, he said,

Oh, the joy of it all. Delighted Joe Harper shows his delight at Hampden after Aberdeen have beaten Celtic in the Scottish Cup Final

Let everyone see the Cup the Dons
won! Aberdeen skipper Martin
Buchan holds up the Scottish Cup
outside Hampden with manager
Eddie Turnbull grasping the
other handle

would be going to avenge the recent 2–1
defeat by Aberdeen at Parkhead. They also
wanted to add the Scottish Cup to their
string of awards—and to ensure they won
the trophy for two years in a row, a distinction which had eluded them for a long time.

For all that, the pundits and the bookies
were convinced Celtic must win because
Celtic were playing with power, finesse,
confidence, versatility and because their
epic deeds spoke for themselves and because
no team in the world could switch styles
with such flair or baffle the opposition with
such slick inter-changes.

There was, however, no sign of inferiority
among the thousands of scarlet-ribboned
supporters from Aberdeen who poured into
Glasgow on the morning of Saturday, 11,
April to pack Hampden's massive stands and
towering terraces. They might have been
out-numbered by the legions in green and
white—but they were proud of their team

and just as vocal as their rivals in their
encouragement.

They agreed with tough-talking Eddie
Turnbull that Aberdeen could march into
Europe 'through the front door and not the
back'—a reference to the fact that the Dons
were already assured of a place in the
European Cup-winners Cup because League
champions Celtic were in the European
Cup. In 1967 when the teams met in the
final Celtic won 2–0 and Aberdeen received
a back-door entry into Europe. As his team
wrapped up their preparations in the
seclusion of Gleneagles, Turnbull hammered
out a promise to the northern fans: 'We want
to go into Europe as Cup-holders, on our
own merits. That's our aim at Hampden.'

And the spectators settled to watch what they expected to be a vivid contrast in styles at Hampden—the explosive Celtic sweeping into attack with the surge of Cossacks, Aberdeen absorbing punishment with the cunning of a veteran middleweight whose crafty gloves and arms protect the vital areas, and then striking venomously on the break.

But we hardly expected the Cup Final of season 1969–70 to be as dramatic as it turned out to be. . . .

A crowd of 108,434 were in Scotland's famous football stronghold when the teams lined up like this:

Aberdeen: Clark; Boel, Murray; Hermiston, McMillan, M. Buchan; McKay, Robb, Forrest, Harper, Graham. 12th man: G. Buchan.

Celtic: Williams; Hay, Gemmell; Murdoch, McNeill, Brogan; Johnstone, Wallace, Connelly, Lennox, Hughes. 12th man: Auld.

Referee: R. H. Davidson, Airdrie.

The Aberdeen selection was exciting. The subtle Alex Willoughby, once of Rangers, was out because of injury and so the accent was on youth, with Martin Buchan, only 21, the captain, and 20-year-old Derek McKay, hero of a Cinderella story, on the right wing and 17-year-old Arthur Graham on the left.

All three soon showed the courageous audacity of youth. In the opening seconds, McKay was challenging Tommy Gemmell, then Graham forced a corner—and, at the other end, Buchan quickly showed he was an inspiring captain, covering beautifully.

Aberdeen kept the eager Celts at arms-length at the start and the champions' run of early goals came to an end. Celtic took a blow when captain Billy McNeill was injured and his ankle obviously pained him.

It was an interesting beginning. But soon Celtic settled and it looked a matter of time until they scored.

Then it was that the first of the afternoon's sensational incidents had the fans in an uproar.

Hardly half an hour had been played. Celtic took a breather and the alert Aberdeen went into an attack. There seemed little danger, however, when McKay, who had been Aberdeen's matchwinner extraordinary in the cup run, shot into a ruck of players. The ball struck a Celtic player, Bobby Murdoch, went past and it looked as though the Dons would take a corner.

It's that daring 'keeper again. Bobby Clark makes another good save, this time from Billy McNeill

Then, to the surprise of everyone at Hampden, it was observed that referee Davidson—Scotland's lone representative in the World Cup finals in Mexico—was signalling for a penalty kick. He had come to the conclusion that Murdoch had armed the ball in the area. Celtic protested heatedly that the handling, if it were such, was accidental, so heatedly that Gemmell was booked. But the referee would have none of it. Joe Harper stroked the ball past Evan Williams with delicate artistry and the Dons were a goal up and the Celtic fans were furious and the Celtic players upset.

That incident occurred in 26 minutes and four minutes later there was another furious outburst from the Celtic fans.

Goalkeeper Bobby Clark and Bobby Lennox were facing each other. The keeper had been having trouble clearing. This time the ball was safely in Clark's hands. Suddenly the ball dropped, was on the ground, was in the net as Lennox prodded it there.

Celtic jubilation was quickly silenced, though. Referee Davidson decided Lennox had knocked the ball out of Clark's grasp. This time Jimmy Johnstone protested— and he, too, was cautioned.

Then came the third blow to Celtic. Lennox was speeding in on goal when Buchan brought him tumbling down. Referee Davidson made signs that Lennox had dived. Certainly it looked like a penalty but Mr. Davidson was firm in his decision again.

From that moment on the writing was on the wall for Celtic. Never did they regain their composure, never did they reveal the brilliant teamwork or the flash of genius that had bejewelled their play on the big occasions so often.

And the Dons took courage. They became more confident, playing with zest and style.

The defence was magnificent, with young skipper Buchan playing outstanding football, covering miles of territory to block the middle of the path to Celtic, and doing it with astounding composure.

Danish back Henning Boel was first-class, too, Tommy McMillan a formidable stopper, George Murray another hero. And Jim Hermiston and Davie Robb were always willing to backtrack to strengthen the defence barrier.

Celtic, however, did not lack bravery. Yet though they attacked and attacked so much in the second half they seldom put Clark in real danger.

So Celtic were caught as so many teams have been caught—by the counter-attack as they gambled on all-out attack for victory. But they were never at their best, simply because Aberdeen refused to let them release their Niagras of wondrous football, hitting them hard and often, never giving them peace or time to plan.

And then, with Celtic coming to the conclusion they would never score, came a fantastic climax, in which three goals were put in the net within the space of seven minutes.

Celtic had just brought on the wily Bertie Auld in a late effort to try to pierce the red gallants in the northern defence. The general of the line had replaced John Hughes with 18 minutes to go and Celtic were driving for the equaliser as hard as they had done during the entire match when Aberdeen broke down the right.

It was a classical move. McKay parted to Harper, who sent Forrest on. The former Rangers leader, at his snappy best, shot and Williams could only parry the ball and McKay was left to drive into the empty net.

Again the Celts hit back. Again they showed their courage. But again Aberdeen showed their defensive class, though they

A tense moment at Hampden—but Aberdeen goalkeeper Bobby Clark saves

were lucky when a Lennox shot shaved the post.

But, with two minutes to go, Lennox got the goal he deserved, a thundering shot from a Wallace pass, which Clark valiantly but vainly tried to stop high in the air.

Any faint hope the Celtic fans had of their team pulling the final out of the fire vanished when Harper broke down the right, cut the ball in and McKay blasted home from short range to make the astonishing score 3–1 for Aberdeen. A dramatic finish indeed to a sensational final.

So it was a fourth time lucky for gallant Aberdeen at Hampden. Beaten in three previous finals by Celtic, they deserved their victory in the end, despite the tremendous controversy in the match.

Certainly it was a day Derek McKay would never forget.

And if the Scottish Cup abounds with fairytales, the rags-to-riches story of young Derek tops the Hans Christian Andersen pop parade.

The winger who had been thrown on the soccer scrapheap by Dundee, who gave him a free, capped an incredible comeback at Hampden when the Dons brought the cup back to Pittodrie for the first time in 23 years.

And what a part he played in Aberdeen's cup run. It was McKay, given his break when influenza hit the side before the quarter-final tie with Falkirk at Brockville, who scored the only goal.

It was McKay who again got the winning goal at Muirton against Kilmarnock in the semi-final. And, of course, the McKay magic brought him two goals against Celtic.

It had been an epic day, too, for Arthur Graham and there was a poignant moment amid the Aberdeen celebrations after the final at Gleneagles. Young Arthur, playing in only his fifth senior game, offered chief scout Bobby Calder his newly-won medal.

Seventeen-year-old Arthur said: 'I wanted to show Bobby my appreciation for discovering me and helping me in my career. When I signed for the Dons I promised him my first medal but I never thought it would come so soon.

Bobby Calder, the man whose signings of young stars have contributed significantly to Aberdeen's triumphs, said: 'Naturally, I didn't take the medal but it was a magnificent, unselfish gesture. I told Arthur that seeing him play as he did against Celtic— the club I pipped to sign him—was reward enough for me.'

Jock Stein also praised Aberdeen and said it was a good thing for Scottish football —as it really was—that the Dons had taken the cup.

It was a pity that the refereeing decisions, which will be bitterly remembered for years to come by Celtic fans, clouded the final.

For Aberdeen deserved great credit for their remarkable performance. They played in a modern manner and the style set by manager Turnbull, who as a player blended perfectly the old with the new, succeeded sensationally.

Their style may not be the most attractive but it is the style adopted nowadays by most of the successful teams. One of their great assets is resiliency and they showed in the final how easily they could absorb punishment without taking a bruise. Their defenders were quick and strong in the tackle, bewilderingly fast in covering, and adept in throwing a net across their goal.

Their other asset was even more devastating—the ability to break quickly and pound into the vitals of the Celtic defence.

Celtic were an outwitted team long before the finish. Aberdeen deserved the congratulations. They were worthy winners and surely that epic victory will put the Dons back at the top of the class—where they belong.

A nasty moment for the Celtic defence as Jim Forrest, of Aberdeen, gets his head to a cross

Sad night at San Siro

THE noise in the huge San Siro stadium in Milan was ear-splitting. There were only 52,000 spectators present—but from the din you might have thought the ground was packed to its 90,000 capacity.

The only trouble for Scots was that the din was being made mainly by a delirious corps of Dutchmen, blowing frenziedly into their trumpets.

It was the night of 6 May 1970, the biggest night in football, the night of the final of the European Cup.

It turned into the saddest night Celtic had ever known.

Yet only a few hours before, Celtic hopes had never been higher. They were the hottest favourites the European Cup Final had ever known. Few people outside Rotterdam gave Feyenoord a chance.

Everyone thought Celtic would become the first British club to win the European Cup for the second time—and win it in style, Celtic style, by using Scotland's favourite and most devastating weapon— real, live wingers.

Celtic were confident indeed—and why not, having beaten Leeds United, pride of England, Fiorentina, Benfica and Basle on the way to the San Siro?

Feyenoord's record, too, was good—they had beaten Reykjavik of Iceland, A.C. Milan, Vorwearts and Legia Warsaw—but nearly every expert in the world tipped Celtic, expecting the Scottish champions to bubble with daring raids, audacious assaults and imaginative overlaps.

Alas, Celtic reserved their worst per-formance of the season for the biggest game of the season—and, as the Scots who had travelled in their thousands filed away silently at the end a sea of waving red and white flags—the Feyenoord colours—sig-nalled disaster for the Parkhead club.

For the gallant, powerful Dutch beat all the odds and became the new European champions, fully deserving their colossal triumph, even though Celtic were defeated only 2–1 in extra time, for they proved a fitter, more sophisticated and certainly stronger side than the Scots.

Celtic had never endured a more tragic night. They never found their rhythm, never discovered the way to beat the Feyenoord defence.

It was never an epic European Cup Final and the blow for Celtic was that the team which had so roundly trounced Leeds in the semi-final would have beaten the good but hardly world-class Dutch.

Celtic, however, never rose to the big occasion and disappointed their vast sup-port.

What went wrong?

Excuses could be made that the husky Dutch were at times over-robust in their tackles, that Jimmy Johnstone, the little winger on whom Celtic pinned such high hopes, was badly hit once or twice and turned into a shadow of his real self.

That would not be fair. Feyenoord were strong but Celtic had met stronger sides. Johnstone was fouled, true, but most times he was cleverly beaten by fine defenders.

No, the truth was that Celtic allowed

Jubilation in Milan . . . Feyenoord, the new champions of Europe

themselves to become frustrated, to falter in face of superior Dutch courage, skill and power.

Feyenoord showed great determination, moved the ball neatly if slowly and made more chances than Celtic. In the Austrian ace, Franz Hasil, they had the most brilliant player on the field, a dominating middle man who could defend and still find time to come upfield and shoot. Indeed, Hasil was the main danger man to Celtic and his influence spread right through the team, which started worriedly and finished in complete command.

Celtic never commanded the middle and Bobby Murdoch and Bertie Auld failed to stamp their authority on the game. George Connelly, who came on for the tiring Auld, tried hard but failed to make much impression on the trend of play.

Yet . . . how different it all might have been.

Celtic started well enough and when Tommy Gemmell scored a spectacular goal from a cute back-heeled free-kick from Murdoch in 29 minutes it seemed that Celtic's dream was coming true.

It seemed Celtic's reading of the game was right, that the Dutch would be upset and anxious. So they were—for about 20 seconds!

Then Feyenoord hit back fiercely. And two minutes later they equalised.

It was a shocking goal to give away. From a foul the ball was lobbed into the heart of the Celtic defence. Billy McNeill did not clear properly and Feyenoord skipper Isreal had room and time to head slowly into the net from a post.

So Celtic were demoralised. They began to disintegrate. Feyenoord gained in confidence as they realised, almost with astonishment, that Celtic were anything but the great team they had imagined and at times they were almost contemptuous in their slow passing. But while you could call them strolling players, they had to be given credit for the effectiveness of their style and the success of their attack.

Sagging Celtic were never allowed to get back into the game.

And yet it appeared Celtic would hold out. They played for the draw which would give them the reprieve—for surely they could not play so badly again. Yet Feyenoord were unlucky, missing chance after chance.

For instance, Hasil the Great hit the post,

then the bar, and Evan Williams, one of the few Celtic successes, made valiant saves when all seemed lost.

But Feyenoord received their just reward in the 116th minute of the match, in the extra time which had proved more exciting than the preceding 90 minutes and in which John Hughes had nearly put Celtic ahead in a solo burst.

But again the tiring Celtic defence were outclassed, out-thought and outplayed. When a free kick came over McNeill could only push the ball away with his hands. It went to the feet of Kindvall, who scored and was immediately swamped by his colleagues. If he hadn't netted, it should have been a penalty.

We knew then it was all over and Celtic had lost and all we could say was . . . What

a tragedy that the real Celtic had not shown up.

There were too many failures, though, for the Scots to have had any hope of beating a Feyenoord team which proved much better than anyone had thought.

In the end, for the Scots, it was the sheer anti-climax much more than the depressing 2–1 result which was so deflating.

We had trekked to Milan confident that victory was a certainty for Celtic. And Celtic had failed miserably to reveal true form.

Indeed, the reason for the defeat was that Milan was Lisbon in reverse.

Said manager Jock Stein sadly: 'We beat ourselves. You cannot win with 80 per cent of the team off form. We went out expecting things to happen. That was wrong. The Dutch went out and made things happen. We did not stretch them as we thought we would. It was something special for Feyenoord. For us it seemed to be just an ordinary game. But it is not the end of the world for Celtic. The defeat will not break us—indeed it might make us.'

Jock was right. Celtic would rise. But they had to take to heart the lesson that in a European Cup, especially in the Final, there are no poor opponents. In Lisbon, it was Celtic who were eager, all out for glory against the experienced Inter-Milan. In the San Siro stadium, Feyenoord were the hungry team, blunting all the Celtic attacks.

Now Celtic's aim was . . . to play again in another Lisbon . . .

Teams at Milan:

Celtic: Williams; Hay, Gemmell; Murdoch, McNeill, Brogan; Johnstone, Wallace, Hughes, Auld, Lennox. Sub: Connelly.

Feyenoord: Graafland; Romeijns, Laseroms, Isreal, Van Duivenbode; Jansen, Hasil, Van Hanegam; Wery, Kindvall, Moulijn. Sub: Haak.

Referree: Concetto Lo Bello, Italy.

New treatment for a goal scorer . . . Kindvall is hoisted shoulder high after snatching Feyenoord's winning European Cup goal

Robbery at Hampden

THE roar of anger might have been heard in Berlin or Bonn. And every Scot packed into the huge crowd of 137,438 at Hampden on 25 April, 1970, was going berserk with rage. The English fans merely blushed and German referee Gerd Schulenberg, surely the most benevolent official in football, just smiled paternally and carried on.

It was the 20th minute of the grim international between Scotland and England and Scotland's gallant, makeshift team were coping almost casually with all the despondent world champions could throw at them and, given comfortable supremacy in the middle of the field, the boys in blue were well on top, ruthlessly thrusting the ball towards the uneasy English defence.

The crowd loved it, loved to see the whiteshirts so much out of it. But the goals weren't coming and that was explained by a combination of bad luck, a lack of instant sharpness in finishing—and bad refereeing.

Then came the worst decision Hampden has seen for many a day. Once again the Scots mounted a fierce attack. Once again Colin Stein, the Ranger back to top form, was demoralising the English defence. He strode almost contemptuously past the towering Brian Labone.

The worried centre-half lashed out, missed the ball—and sent Stein tumbling down on the damp, green grass. 'Penalty', howled every Scot.

It seemed a blatant foul, a glaring penalty. If it wasn't, the laws of the game have surely ceased to have any meaning. But Herr Schulenberg, who said afterwards he thought Stein had taken a dive, merely shook his head—and waved play on. It was one of the most insupportable decisions Hampden has ever seen and the crowd were justifiably angry.

It was, perhaps, the turning point. Some of the heart was knocked out of the Scots. They fought on bravely after the cruel disappointment and almost immediately John O'Hare and Jimmy Johnstone had the English defence in spinning confusion again. Inevitably the ball came across Gordon Banks's goal and Stein seemed set to sweep it into the net. This time, alas, it bounced crazily off his foot and soared over the bar.

Scotland seemed to feel fate was against them. It was. And so, too, was the referee. His charity to the world champions, who were about to set off to defend their title in Mexico, made the crowd sigh.

There were two other loud penalty claims. One came 15 minutes from the end when Tommy Gemmell crashed in a shot which Bobby Moore seemed to handle. The other arrived with five minutes left for play. Nobby Stiles rapped John O'Hare's heels from the rear. Not all the Scottish appeals nor the frenzied anger of the crowd could move the referee.

And, oh how frustrating it was to see the bold Scots robbed of a reward they so richly deserved. In terms of pure football, aggressive intent and will to win, the new-look Scottish side played England right off Hampden.

In the second half, for instance, all the lively soccer came from Scotland. Wee Jimmy Johnstone was nippy, clever, fast, despite a series of fouls against him. And there was one fine chance set up when Stein, always persistent, forced the ball away from Moore. The ball went to O'Hare and the Derby man beat Banks to it wide of the goal but he hit the side netting and the chance was gone.

Then England's anxious team manager, Sir Alf Ramsay, made a surprising change. He brought on Alan Mullery, a midfield player, for Peter Thomson, who had been making the Scottish defence run in a few breaks. It was an admission by Sir Alf that he would be content to settle for a draw.

That move certainly took some of the pressure off the England goal for with four men in midfield they could hold the ball there, pinning down the game as a form of defence.

And yet Scotland still made chances. There was the time Johnstone broke into the fixed England plan when he was sent away on the right by his Celtic colleague, David Hay, surely the discovery of the year. His cross passed through a ruck of players, needing only a touch for a goal. Alas, no one was there but the England apprehension about the lively little winger was shown in a tough double tackle by two defenders which had the crowd howling again.

Again England's goal escaped when Johnstone pushed the ball through the centre defence and left Stein with a chance. Colin shot, Banks dived to save and

almost immediately leaped high to take Johnstone's hook shot—a magnificent exhibition of acrobatic artistry by a world-class goalkeeper.

But time was running out. The Scottish players knew it and the crowd knew it and they urged on their team with renewed vigour. With four minutes to go, the brilliant Bobby Moncur, general of the Scottish defence, had to go off, suffering from double vision, and Alan Gilzean came on. And still the Scots pressed—in vain.

And there were only two minutes to go when tragedy, it seemed, struck the Scots. In an isolated raid, Geoff Hurst headed into the Scottish net and there was a stunned silence, followed by a sigh of relief which was just like a boiler bursting when a linesman signalled offside and referee agreed. It would have been a ludicrous result had that goal been allowed to stand.

So the game ended frustratingly in a 0–0 draw—and that was the first time in 98 years such a result had been recorded. It was back in 1872, at the Partick ground in Glasgow, that Scotland and England met for the first time in football combat. They didn't manage to score a goal between them.

But all the honours of 1970 went to Scotland. Even Sir Alf Ramsey, no lover of the tartan, admitted that afterwards. He said: 'England were more than a little fortunate to get away with it.'

And as the crowd filed sadly away from the massive bowl of Hampden they were all saying: 'We were robbed.'

And the mystery of the referee's decision kept them talking late into the night. There was another Hampden mystery, as well. It was one the police were trying to solve. For there were thousands of extra spectators at Hampden. The number of tickets printed was—134,000. But the official

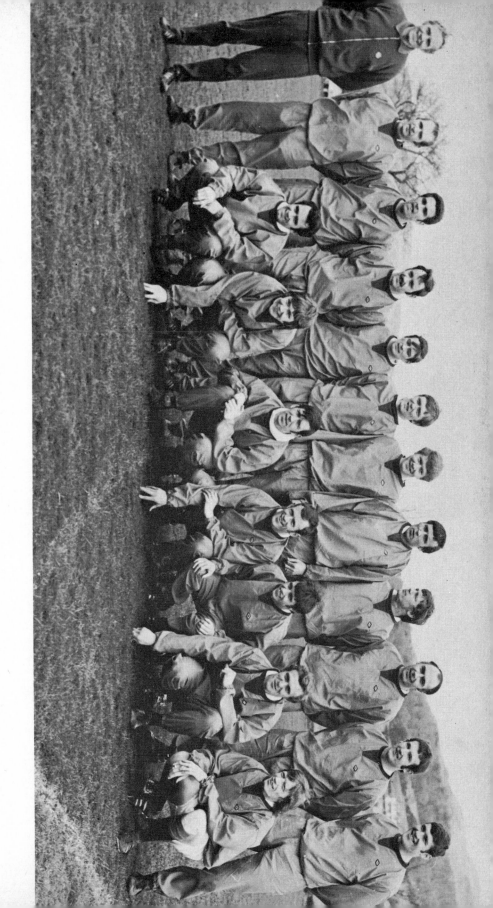

The bright Scots who sent this country's prospects soaring sky-high pictured at training at Largs during the home international series. *Back row* (*left to right*): Manager Bobby Brown, trainer Tom McNiven, Bobby Moncur, Jim Cruickshank, John O'Hare, David Hay, Keith McRae, Ronnie McKinnon, Willie Johnston, Alan Gilzean, Billy Dickson, Bobby Clark. *Front row*: Willie Callaghan, John Blackaly, John Greig, Bobby Lennox, Tommy McLean, Colin Stein, Willie Carr. From this pool Scotland can choose a team to put us back on top of the world

Ronnie McKinnon clears in one of the few English raids

Davie Hay fails in a raid on the English goal with Hughes and Stiles in command for once ▶

attendance came to 137,438.

Police said many of the extra fans got in with counterfeit tickets.

But Scottish hearts were high, even though the team finished joint leaders in the British Championship, having scored only one goal, against Ireland.

And our international prospects were bright.

No wonder team manager Bobby Brown was pleased. He had to field teams without great stars such as Billy McNeill, Bobby Murdoch and John Hughes, of Celtic; Billy Bremner and Eddie Gray of Leeds, and Charlie Cooke, of Chelsea, because of injury or club's commitments.

Yet the makeshift side were magnificent against England, having found new confidence following the games against Ireland and Wales.

It's true England were without the

John Greig and Bobby Moore shake hands before the start of the international as German referee Gerd Schulenberg looks on

Happy moment after the
Scotland v. England international
at Hampden. Emlyn Huges of
Liverpool and new Scottish find
Willie Carr, of Coventry,
exchange jerseys

Come fly with me . . . Brian
Labone moves in. Scotland
striker Colin Stein takes off.
But strong claims for a
penalty were turned down
by German referee Gerhard
Schulenberg, and the Scots
had to be content with a
draw

shrewd Bobby Charlton, who was injured on the eve of the match, but they were made to look shabby by the eager Scots, so much so that they no more resembled world champions than Auchenshuggle Primrose and there was a reek of the jungle about some of their methods.

Although there must be concern about the lack of a venomous finishing touch, Scotland's prospects soared sky-high. It was a moral victory over England. And at last it seemed that Scotland had the players and the style and the technique and the courage to make a hit in global football. Of course, the team weren't perfect. Despite the stout-hearted attacking of Stein and O'Hare, there was a lack of snap near goal.

The players need time to become accustomed to the pace of each other—and if they do Scotland can win the new European Nations Championship.

If there were reservations about the attack, there was no doubt that manager Brown had discovered a defence as solid as that of any country in the world.

Jim Cruickshank appeared to have solved the problem which has beset this country for years—goalkeeper. The Hearts man looked good, was good and inspired confidence. And Bobby Moncur is our man for all seasons—the most solid citizen we have found for a long time. His style may not be silky but he seldom made a mistake, read the play brilliantly and brought out the best in his colleagues, especially centre-half Ronnie McKinnon.

Another dazzling find was Billy Dickson, of Kilmarnock, who played with flair and assurance.

Now it is manager Brown's task to polish this fine side. I believe he will stick to the 4–3–3 style, which proved so effective, though perhaps it is a safety-first device, with a 4–2–4 producing more entertainment.

But Brown can ring the changes. He has plenty of variety to call on.

The English agreed. Even the most chauvinistic of their reporters admitted that no goalless draw had ever inflicted more blatant injustice on any team than the Hampden 0–0 result did on a Scotland team who did everything but run the English into the Clyde.

The home international series ended in a three-way tie, with only Ireland failing to share it, but no foreigner who watched the game would have any doubt that the brave Scots are unequalled in Britain.

As Celtic's manager, Jock Stein, who has brought so much honour to Scotland, said after the game: 'This was the game when our international team was born again.'

He was right. The international championship did not matter. What mattered was that at Hampden a feeling among the fans for the international team was rekindled.

Scotland: Cruickshank (Hearts); Gemmell (Celtic), Dickson (Kilmarnock); Greig (Rangers), McKinnon (Rangers), Moncur (Newcastle U.); Johnstone (Celtic), Hay (Celtic), Stein (Rangers), O'Hare (Derby Co.), Carr (Coventry City). *Sub.:* Gilzean (Spurs).

England: Banks (Stoke); Newton (Everton), Hughes (Liverpool); Stiles (Manchester United), Labone (Everton), Moore (West Ham United); Thomson (Liverpool), Ball (Everton), Astle (West Brom), Hurst (West Ham), Peters (Spurs). *Sub.:* Mullery (Spurs).

Referee: G. Schulenberg, West Germany.

Henry Hall, St. Johnstone's lively
goal-scorer, takes it easy for once

The one goal that really matters

By
HENRY HALL
St Johnstone F.C.

JUST because I have scored exactly 50
goals in fewer than two seasons with St.
Johnstone—and finished top of the pile last
term—doesn't mean I can sit back now and
let things take their own course.

Anyone who feels that I have achieved
all I can in football is certainly 'way off the
mark'. I'll tell you why.

Firstly, any player who goes on to the
field week after week without ambition,
without the urge to do even better, would
be just as well staying in the dressing-room.
He is no longer any good to himself or his
club.

Secondly, out of these 50 goals, I still
haven't scored the one that really matters—
the goal that will give Saints a trophy, a
title or at least take them into Europe.

Whenever I tend to forget what football
is all about I remind myself of one game . . .

and promise myself that I'll try even harder in future.

That game is the League Cup final we played against Celtic at Hampden last October. That game is an inspiration to me and the rest of the staff at Muirton.

It was St. Johnstone's first ever national cup final and my first big match at the famous ground.

I was bitterly disappointed that we lost, with a goal by Bertie Auld before we had even been given time to settle into the strange surroundings and atmosphere.

But it was an experience I loved. It proved to me that there is no place like Hampden on cup final or international day. Now it is one of my ambitions to go back there with St. Johnstone. And, next time I want to be on the winning side.

That defeat by Celtic cost us a place in the Fairs Cup, the second time the rule book had robbed the club of European football.

A few months earlier, we had finished sixth in the League and seemed certain to qualify. But the Fairs Cup committee decided to accept only three entries from Scotland instead of four.

When we met Celtic, we were just 90 minutes away from our ambition. But again we were robbed by the rule book because the committee refuse to admit runners-up in the League Cup, even though Celtic were to go on to qualify again for the European Cup.

The people of Perth proved by their support for the Scottish Cup semi-final between Aberdeen and Kilmarnock that they will turn out for top-class football. It's up to everyone at Muirton to give them more opportunities to see the best there is.

Maybe the chance will come soon. Certainly, I think we are capable of beating most sides when we hit our top form.

I think we have too many good players to stay out of Europe for long. All we need is a

Bill McCarry, of St. Johnstone

little more consistency—and we can achieve that by working just a bit harder at our game.

It will only be when we do get right to the top that I shall start feeling that I have finally achieved something worth while.

Still, I suppose I can feel reasonably satisfied with my career so far. And for that I have a lot to thank my old club, Stirling Albion.

But for them I could easily have faded right out of the game. When I was just 17, I was provisionally signed by Dundee.

I played only one reserve game for them, against Celtic at Parkhead, before Bob Shankly left the club and Bobby Ancell took over at Dens Park.

The new boss decided to give me a free transfer—without even seeing me play. Just when it seemed I might be set for success, I was back with my junior club, Kirkintilloch Rob Roy.

Fortunately, I had the sense to realise that good players are sometimes freed when a managerial change takes place, such as the one at Dens.

I decided that the only thing to do was get on with trying to improve my game with Rob Roy. It worked. In no time at all, Albion came along with an offer and I went to Annfield.

I had three good seasons with them, finishing top scorer there on one occasion, before I was transferred to Muirton.

The fee of £15,000 isn't big by modern standards, but it was for Saints. Their fans expected something special for that kind of money, and I hope I haven't let them down.

I am certain we would have achieved more by now but for a bad run of injuries at times. We must be the only club in the country who had a whole forward line injured last season.

When our luck changes, I am sure the fortunes of St. Johnstone will also change.

St. Johnstone skipper, Benny Rooney

Player of the Year

PAT STANTON, of Hibernian, was chosen as Scotland's player of the year 1970 by the Scottish Football Writers' Association—and no-one more deserved the honour.

The loyal Hibernian follows in the footsteps of Billy McNeill, John Greig, Ronnie Simpson, Gordon Wallace and Bobby Murdoch and he was given his trophy at the writers' annual dinner in Glasgow.

The modest, unassuming Patrick Gordon Stanton is an inspiration and a glowing example to any aspiring footballer. Not only is he a tremendous player, for Scotland and for his club, he is everything a manager could desire.

And at the dinner no-one clapped more heartily than Celtic manager Jock Stein when Pat received the player of the year award.

It was when Jock was manager of Dunfermline Athletic that he nearly signed Stanton. One of his scouts told him: 'Go and see this boy Pat Stanton, who plays for Bonnyrigg Rose'. Jock went to see Pat as soon as he could. It took his experienced eye only a minute or so to decide Stanton was a man of great talent. As soon as the junior game finished Jock made his approach. Too late.

Pat told Mr. Stein he had already promised to join Hibs. And there was nothing to be done about it.

Pat had given his word. That was his bond.

But Jock Stein's luck turned. He became manager of Hibernian—and, of course, fell heir to the player he'd wanted a year before.

Pat is a versatile player. He is a stand-out as a sweeper and he is equally effective as a linkman. Soon he must become a regular in the Scotland team. His luck was out when he could not join the Scotland pool at Largs for the 1970 home international championship series because he had been ill. Otherwise he would surely have played against England.

Although he is only 25, Pat has enjoyed many great moments in football, his greatest triumph being when Hibs won 5–0 against Naples in a second leg Fairs Cities Cup tie at Easter Road . . . after losing 4–1 in Italy.

Another game he relished was the League international against England at Newcastle when the Scots won 3–1. It was Pat's first cap.

The player Stanton most admires is Bobby Charlton, of England and Manchester United. What else could you expect? Stanton is also a brilliant footballer—and a great sportsman.

Let's hope he has many years to play for Hibernian—and Scotland!

THE ELITE OF THE ELITE

IF YOU were a manager and had the choice of the world's greatest players, how would you go about picking the team of your dreams?

Would you pin your faith in great artists? Would you make star quality your only qualification?

Or would you try to blend your team?

I pose these questions because last season 80 international football writers, including myself, from 35 different countries took part in 'World Sports' poll to select the best World team in the past 20 years. The writers couldn't vote for players from their own countries and the final team selected was:

Lev Yashin (USSR); Djalma Santos (Brazil), Giacinto Facchetti (Italy); Josef Boszik (Hungary), Billy Wright (England), Franz Beckenbauer (West Germany); Stanley Matthews (England), Pele (Brazil), Alfredi di Stefano (Argentina), Ferenc Puskas (Hungary), Bobby Charlton (England).

As 'World Sports' said . . . 'They are the pick of the best . . . the elite of the elite.'

I agree. After all, I helped to choose some of them.

But is this team necessarily the best *team* the world has known from 1950 until the present day?

I do not ask this question in a state of pique because no Scots are represented. Indeed, this poll must have shaken all of us who reckoned Scotland produces the best players in the world; for only one Scot was mentioned, Jim Baxter, of Rangers, who gained three votes.

No, I ask because a team of all-stars doesn't necessarily bring the most successful side. Modern teams must be blended; modern teams must put teamwork before individual ability. And I have the feeling that the team of all the talents, astoundingly good as it might well have been if all the greats had played together, might not have been as brilliant as the line-up suggests.

Stars can be temperamental. Stars can take the huff. Stars can refuse to co-operate with lesser mortals, never mind giants of similar stature.

And can you see a forward line of Matthews, Pele, di Stefano, Puskas and Charlton blending? Can you imagine any of these being merely a fetcher and carrier?

I would, I admit, dearly love to have seen this attack in action . . . it might have been sensational. But it might also have been a flop.

And I wonder what Matthews would have said if he had suddenly been waved away as Facchetti, for instance, decided to go into overlapping action down the right wing?

Whether sheer class, brilliant artistry, individual genius would have told in the end, whether this eleven would have been the greatest team we have ever known . . . well, it's all a matter for conjecture.

Many of us who are turning grey— because of age, not because of modern football!—will undoubtedly believe that an old-fashioned system was best and, therefore, magnificent wingers such as Matthews and Charlton, supported by scheming inside-forwards such as Pele and Puskas and spearheaded by that flashing centre-forward, di Stefano, taking part in the dearly beloved but passé 2-3-5 formation, could never be surpassed for glorious enterprise and fascinating football.

But I must be fair. Present-day football may not be as exhilarating as the old-fashioned play—that is, to veterans who look at the past through the rosy glow of retrospect. But I must confess that modern teams would beat practically any of those of the past, even a team composed of such outstanding players as 'World Sports' global eleven.

For there is more planning in football now. Players are stronger and fitter and faster and they can control the ball at speeds which would have amazed the old-timers, who used to bleat at colleagues who passed the ball too fiercely. More thought is put into tactics. Great players are still needed; indeed, they are still with us. But mavericks aren't wanted; players have their roles delegated and they must stick to them for the good of the team.

That is why I believe the 'reserve' team in the 'World Sports' magazine poll might have been more successful than the 'first eleven'. For it is more modern, more likely to adopt the new tactics, while still retaining players of the top class. This eleven was:

Gordon Banks (England); Nilton Santos (Brazil), Karl-Heinz Schnellinger (West Germany); Josef Masopust (Czechoslovakia), Ernst Ocwirk (Austria), Bobby Moore (England); Garrincha (Brazil), Didi (Brazil), Eusebio (Portugal), George Best (N. Ireland), Francisco Gento (Spain).

Now, I wouldn't be as arrogant as to say that Scotland could have produced a team during the past 20 years to match either of these two global elevens.

Sometimes we are too partisan in Scotland, too inclined to believe, despite disaster after disaster, that we are the greatest in football, refusing to believe that other countries have outstripped us in thought and ability.

But I am confident enough to assert that Scotland could have produced over the last two decades an eleven which would hold its head up in any company, an eleven which would gain fame among the 'mods', an eleven which could combine old-fashioned Scottish soccer with the best of the current trend.

Now, some years ago, I picked this as the best team Scotland could produce:

Jimmy Cowan (Morton); George Young (Rangers), Sammy Cox (Rangers); Bobby Evans (Celtic), Davie Meiklejohn (Rangers), Jimmy McMullan (Manchester City); Willie Waddell (Rangers), Jimmy Mason (Third Lanark), Hughie Gallacher (Newcastle United), Alex James (Preston North End) and Alan Morton (Rangers).

I still submit that this would have been a super side. But as football has progressed since the time I made this my selection and as many of the players were not in action during the past 20 years, I must change my mind.

And my team from Scotland of the past 20 years would be packed with players who could stand up to modern pressures, who could sublimate their individual skills to the good of the team and who would not be lost in what is sometimes a soccer jungle called 'modern professionalism', which is a term, to cover a multitude of fouls, jabs, pushes shoves, pulls and other illegal tactics.

My team, then.

Bill Brown (Spurs); Alex Parker (Falkirk), Tommy Gemmell (Celtic); Billy Bremner (Leeds United), Willie Woodburn

(Rangers), Jim Baxter (Rangers); Jimmy Johnstone (Celtic), John White (Spurs), Lawrie Reilly (Hibs), Billy Steel (Dundee) and John Hughes (Celtic).

I feel this team would have blended superbly, would have been tough as well as talented, would have fitted perfectly into a real team, to play not for their own glory but for Scotland.

You may say: Why Woodburn? Willie, I know, didn't play in the new era. But he still played for Scotland in the early 1950s and I am convinced that had he been in action today he would have been hailed all over the world as the No. 1 centre-half.

And how sorry I am that we will never see those fine Celtic wingers, Johnstone and Hughes, helped by magnificent inside-men such as White and Steel.

Anyhow, it's all an exercise, this selecting of teams we can never see. But a fascinating exercise for all that.

Meet some of the Elite

Here are some of the players who would grace any World XI.

The elegant Jim Baxter, of Rangers, the only Scot mentioned in a world voting contest for a global eleven

John Hughes of Celtic (*right*), with colleague Bobby Lennox behind him. Hughes would be in Taylor's Scotland XI

One of the great Continental players—Sandro Mazzola, toast of Inter-Milan not so long ago

Billy Steel, in Hugh Taylor's opinion, Scotland's outstanding inside forward. Bill starred with Morton and Dundee, among other clubs

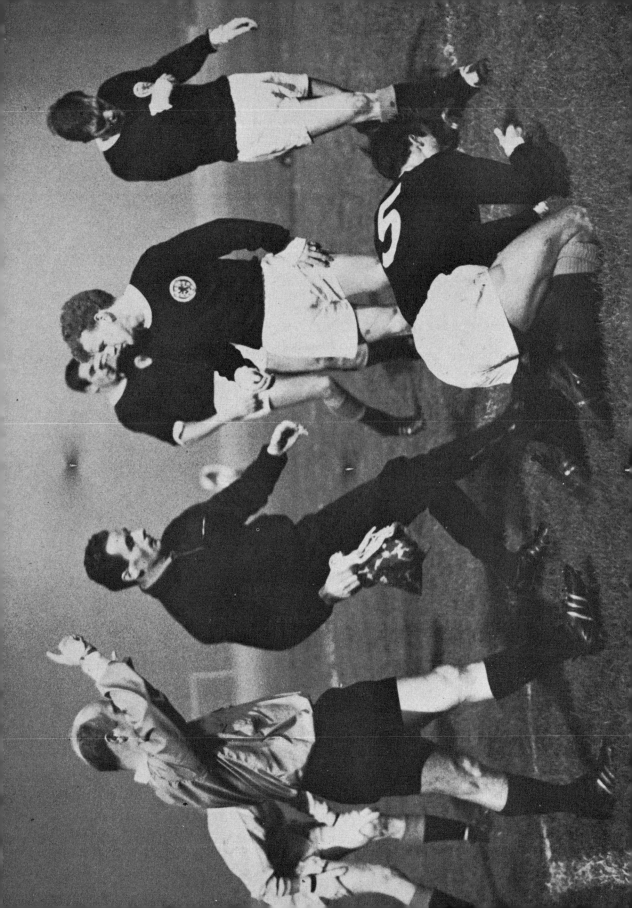

Among the top England stars are Martin Peters (West Ham and Spurs) and Bobby Charlton (Manchester United), seen here after a Scotland v. England match with John Hughes and Tommy Gemmel, of Celtic

Billy Bremner, Scotland's captain, one of our top stars, watches Walter McCrae, now Kilmarnock manager, as the trainer runs to help the injured Ronnie McKinnon, of Rangers

The team I most want to beat

**By
ROSS MATHIE**

Kilmarnock F.C.

THE biggest disappointment I had last season—my first as a full-time senior—was Kilmarnock's failure to beat Aberdeen in the Scottish Cup semi-final at Muirton.

Every side feels awful about a semi-final defeat; it's probably the worst stage to be beaten in the competition. There's a chance you might be remembered as beaten finalists, but not much that anyone can recall the two teams who failed to make the final.

But, for me, there was more than just the usual reasons. I had an extra incentive to beat Aberdeen . . .

Why? Well, every player likes to put one over his old team, and I'm no exception.

And if the name Ross Mathie, of Aberdeen, seems strange to you, I can assure you that for eight months it was a fact.

It was back in 1964 that I signed as a teenager for Aberdeen from the amateur club Motherwell Bridge Works, that soccer nursery which produced those great players for Liverpool, Ian St. John and Bobby Graham.

However, because my amateur club were heavily involved in local competitions it was decided—after I had spent a week training at Pittodrie—that I would stay with them, and be called up at the end of the season.

Unfortunately for me before I could join the full-time staff at Aberdeen they had changed managers. And the man who had signed me, Tommy Pearson, left and Eddie Turnbull took over.

Mr. Turnbull axed a long list of the provisional signings that season, and I was one of them. It seemed to me, as a mere 17-year-old, that the end of the road had come for me in football . . . but there was worse to follow.

Cambuslang Rangers wanted to take me into the juniors, but because I had signed straight from an amateur side to Aberdeen, the Scottish F.A. refused to let me join them.

So it was right back to where I started, with the Motherwell Bridge team, and I stayed there for a few seasons, until the S.F.A. lifted the ban on players, such as myself, joining a junior club.

And the first club on my doorstep to ask me to join them were . . . Cambuslang Rangers!

I was nearly 23 when I signed for Kilmarnock. That's old by present-day standards when many First Division clubs like to bring kids on to their staff at around sixteen, and groom them from there.

Yet I don't regret the spell I had with Cambuslang. I know the juniors are not regarded as being too fashionable nowadays, but I still think they give any young player valuable experience. Certainly I am not unhappy now, looking back, that the venture with Aberdeen did not come off, for it gave me time to mature my game.

The man who spotted me for Kilmarnock was Willie McLean, the brother of my team-mates, Tommy and Jim, and then scouting for the club.

But there was a snag when Kilmarnock wanted me on trial. Cambuslang were still vitally interested in the Scottish Junior Cup, and I think they were getting a bit tired of senior teams wanting their men for matches.

Here is Ross Mathie (*right*) with his partner, Eddie Morrison, in Kilmarnock's deadly double striking act

Kilmarnock's brilliant little goalkeeper, Sandy McLaughlan

So Kilmarnock were told that if they wanted me, then they would have to take the whole team on trial.

That's how the entire Cambuslang side played Kilmarnock Reserves one night in a closed-doors match. And the most surprised player on the park when I was offered signing terms after the game was myself.

I had not finished work until 6 p.m.— hardly the best preparation for such a game —and frankly I was not too happy with the way I played.

However, I was happy to accept the chance, and I must say it has worked out better than my first senior attempt.

PROMOTION

Really, the people who have made it all possible are the back-room staff at Rugby Park who have helped me reach fitness, and my team-mates on the park, who have aided me to these goals.

I played three games in the reserves at the start of last season, and then I was promoted to the League side.

I don't think I really appreciated what a vast difference there is between that standard and League football.

For the first few matches I was on my legs for the last 15 minutes, desperately hoping the referee would blow the final whistle.

I managed to overcome that, and I was lucky enough to keep my place to play— and score—in Kilmarnock's three ties in the European Fairs Cup against Zurich of Switzerland, CSK Slavia of Bulgaria and Dynamo Bachau of Rumania.

These matches were eye-openers for me. They introduced me to problems in football I only suspected existed.

The dashing Ross Mathie in action against Rangers, with Morrison up to help

Believe me, sometimes on the terracing you don't see everything. I thought I knew a few of the dodges defences use to stop forwards, but some of the Continental sides added to my knowledge.

The big disappointment in that competition was our elimination by the Rumanian side, Bachau. I thought they were a very good side—even though they were later beaten by Arsenal.

Still, I am hoping there will be plenty more chances in these competitions. For I believe you really can learn from the experience of playing in them.

There was always something new to learn in every match during my first season, and I hope I was able to profit by it.

The defence which impressed me most was Celtic's—they obviously don't become champions for nothing.

But the centre-half I rated the tops was Jim Black, of Hibs, a very clever player indeed.

I would not have been surprised if I had not been given a first-team chance until maybe halfway through the season. But when I did get it, as I say, I owe a lot to my team-mates, particularly Tommy McLean, for all the service they gave me.

I'm just glad I was able to get a few goals to help repay them!

Kilmarnock at training. *Left to right:* **Andy King, Allan MacDonald and Jackie McGrory. Starting the sprint is Rugby Park backroom boy, John Murdoch**

THE LIGHTS OF HOME ARE BRIGHTEST

By
Jim Hendry

DUNDEE UNITED F.C.

CALL me the kid who stayed at home . . , the boy who turned aside the lure of the big city and the bright lights.

When I was playing for Dundee St. Francis Boys' Club a couple of years ago, I heard plenty of talk from teammates about offers to join Manchester United, Leeds and Spurs—not to mention the other big-name clubs in England.

But, when my chance came, I turned down Huddersfield Town to join Dundee United, the club from Tannadice Street not a couple of miles from my home.

And I can say in all honesty that I haven't regretted that decision for one moment of my career. Indeed, my advice to anyone tempted to go south is to think twice, to think of the club just around the corner or just down the road.

After all, I wonder where I would be now if I had decided to join Huddersfield or any of the other clubs who were interested. I certainly doubt if I'd have any experience of European football and around 20,000 miles of jet-set travel behind me at the ripe old age of 20!

In the last year I have become an established member of the first team pool at Tannadice. And this little fish in the big pool has been to many faraway places, including Mexico.

Mind you, there were times when I would have laughed at the idea of making the grade, even on my own doorstep.

Like the sultry, sticky night in London in August 1969 when manager Jerry Kerr decided to give me my big chance in the challenge match against Millwall at the Den.

When the boss told me I was in the side, I was over the moon with excitement. And no wonder. I was only in the party for the pre-season tour of England because top-scorer Kenny Cameron had been hurt in training.

Just 45 minutes later, however, I was back to square one. What should have been the greatest night of my life had turned sour. One tackle . . . one distant crack of breaking bone and my dream of going to the top in football was forgotten.

In the dressing-room at half time I insisted I was all right, that I could go back on for the second half. But when I tried, I collapsed in the tunnel leading to the pitch.

I had fractured a bone in my left foot. The injury meant a night in hospital in London. It's bad enough being in hospital anywhere, but I think I'd just as soon go through a spell with a witch doctor in a mud hut in darkest Africa as go through that again.

I think whoever said that London can be the loneliest city in the world must have spoken those words from the same bed!

The injury couldn't have come at a worse time, and not just because I was so far from home.

The boss had been impressed by my performance before I was injured and had already decided that my future was at left-half.

But what chance did I have with my leg in plaster and so many other fine players challenging for the first team place in that position?

There was Alex Stuart, who had just joined the club from Dundee, Stuart Markland and Wilson Wood. Soon afterwards Billy Higgins, another left-half, joined the club.

Left-half was one position Mr. Kerr didn't have to worry about. So why should he worry about a boy with an iron on his foot?

But he did care, more, I'm sure, than anyone with the big English clubs I could have joined would have cared in similar circumstances. He, and the rest of the training staff, were a tremendous help in coaxing me back to fitness.

Eventually, the boss gave me another chance in a friendly against the American club, Dallas Tornado. I was left out again for the following League game, against Ayr United at Tannadice.

Back again I came, however, against an Inverness Select for our friendly at Kingsmills.

The park was hardly Hampden or Wembley—but don't let anyone ever tell me that. It was there that I really took my first steps towards a comeback and a real career in the game.

We won 10–2. United will probably never win a game so easily. That didn't worry me. I was on the way back and that was all that mattered.

My luck was on the up-and-up, something I had doubted would ever happen as I lay in that hospital in London.

Wilson Wood was still having re-signing problems, Alex Stuart was on the verge of becoming player-manager of Montrose, and Billy Higgins was still waiting for clearance from the South African club he had just left.

I could hardly believe it, but United were actually looking for a regular left-half. I started to believe when the manager told me I was playing against St. Mirren the following Saturday, my League début.

Few people know it, but I went through agony that day in October. Every time an opponent came near me, I thought back to Millwall and the night when my first big chance had ended tragically.

Nothing happened, of course. It proved to me finally that someone up there did like me. My luck had changed completely in three months.

Someone else liked me that day—my boss. He told me so right after we had won the match 3–1.

I had been given the chance to break through to the first team, and he reckoned I had taken it. He showed his confidence by keeping me in the side.

I arrived in the first team during a good League run, when other players could afford a little time to encourage a beginner.

How could I fail? After all, I stepped into a half-back line with Dennis Gillespie and Doug Smith. If you can't settle in with these two you should hang up your boots.

I'll always remember my first season, and the way I crowned it. I scored one of the goals against Raith Rovers in the second last match to make sure that we would qualify for the Fairs Cup.

Around that time, too, everyone at Tannadice was talking about the games we were to play in the close season—and the countries we were to visit . . .

So don't let anyone fool you. Don't let anyone tell you dreams don't come true in football.

If anyone tries, just tell them to get in touch with Jim Hendry at Tannadice Park.

Jim Hendry, Dundee United's
bright young star, shows a group
of interested schoolboys
how it should be done

What's going on here?

Gay and grim, triumphant and tragic, any football season is a kaleidoscope of life. And a football season is not just a cheer of great goals, a terror of relegation or an adoration of title awards.

It has moments of fun, moments of hardship.

And last season was no exception.

Last season had highlights like these . . . times when we asked: What's going on here?

Moment of joy. Celtic goalkeeper Evan Williams does a handstand to celebrate his team's Scottish Cup-tie win over old rivals, Rangers

Stand by for a cup of char! And Hearts are finding Army tea is refreshing. Not that the famous Tynecastle players have joined the Army. Hearts played the soldiers of Redford Barracks at soccer in a training game before a Scottish Cup-tie. Everyone enjoyed it and now manager Johnny Harvey dishes out the tea

Moment of relief (*above*). Airdrie goalkeeper Roddy McKenzie watches a shot go narrowly past. They're hardy warriors in the North of Scotland. Snow doesn't stop our footballing Highlanders. But the snow is cold indeed for Brora 'keeper Davidson as Inverness Caley's Chic Allan scored in this match

Breathtaking . . . that's the only word for this fine save by Dunfermline Athletic goalkeeper, John Arrol

The season showed that Scotland still have brilliant young players (*above*). Here members of the Scotland Under-23 international team have a chat over coffee. They are Tommy McLean and Billy Dickson, of Kilmarnock, Willie Johnston, of Rangers, and whizz-kid Peter Marinello, who went to Arsenal from Hibernian

It's a piggy-back Jim Hermiston would rather have done without. The Aberdeen wing-half was injured in the Scottish Cup semi-final with Kilmarnock at Muirton Park, Perth, and had to be carried off on the broad back of Jim Bonthrone. Jim's consolation was that the Dons won

What the well-dressed substitute wears. Harry Hood, of Celtic, keeps off the chilly air with a tartan rug as he sits in the dug-out with manager Jock Stein at an Old Firm game

A sight defences fear (*left*). Celtic's Billy McNeill comes up for a high cross. This time the centre-half is first to the ball—and it's a goal again. The place: Tannadice. The opposition to Celtic: Dundee United

Certainly Scotland's a chilly country. And
Italian star Di Sisti (*left*) took precautions
when Fiorentina played Celtic in the
European Cup at Parkhead. He had a vest
below his shirt—as we discovered when
he swopped jerseys with Bertie Auld
after the game

Ouch, that was sore! Hibernian
sweeper John Blackley takes a
knock in a tussle with Alec
McDonald, of Rangers

What's going to happen now. Chris Shevlane and John Blackley, of Hibs, keep an eye on former colleague, Colin Stein, of Rangers, as they await a corner kick

That was sore, too (*left*). But Jimmy Johnstone, of Celtic, quickly forgets the pain. For a clearance by an Airdrie defender has hit him—and the ball then rolled into the net

HAMBURG HORROR

Failure and bitter disappointment for Scotland

Colin Stein goes near for Scotland but is beaten by goalkeeper Maier in the World Cup game against West Germany

IT was a fine compliment. And it came from a man who knew what he was talking about. After the match in Hamburg between West Germany and Scotland, the then Brazilian team manager, Joao Saldanha, said: 'Scotland were 100 years ahead of Germany.'

Very nice. Very pleasing. But the brutal truth was that the out-of-date Germans had beaten the futuristic Scots 3–2. And Germany were through to the finals of the World Cup in Mexico. And Scotland were out, finished, beaten, also-rans—once again. And later Saldanha was sacked . . .

We Scots who shed tartan tears weren't really surprised at the defeat. We knew Scotland produced fine players, knew our tactics were good—but we also knew there was a grave weakness in our international team.

WORLD CUP BLUES AGAIN

The big problem was: How to eradicate it.

For the problem, as I see it, is to find a team—and keep it playing in game after game until, like all the most effective modern international combinations, it plays like a club side.

But Scotland, alas, can seldom play the same eleven even twice—for a variety of reasons, including injuries and the withdrawal of Anglos.

This, I maintain, is the real reason for Scotland's lack of success in top-class international football.

This is why Scotland, despite our fame, tradition and resources in brilliant ball players, have not qualified for a World Cup since 1958.

For there is nothing wrong with the quality of the individual players and our little country, which, thanks to Queen's Park's pioneers, invented the passing game and set the pattern for the world to follow, still throws up brilliant talents in profusion.

And our tactics, as the Brazilian boss said, were as modern as tomorrow.

But we cannot field the same eleven time after time.

And the tragic story of Hamburg portrays the ills and problems of Scottish soccer in the World Cup.

* * *

It was October 1969, and once again everything was going wrong for team manager Bobby Brown, diligent, dedicated, and his men. On the day before the match, a day in which our chances took another sad knock because of the withdrawal of Hugh Curran, the new striker from Wolves, down with influenza, optimists in the Scotland party were as scarce as a glimpse of sunshine in the mist-enveloped, brooding seaport of Hamburg.

Earlier, Scotland had been hit by injuries to John Hughes, Bobby Lennox and Eddie McCreadie, And although skipper Billy Bremner was, as always, confident, the framework of the side had been weakened by the sad series of withdrawals.

So, alas, on the night of 22 October, after the dramatic match in the Volkspark Stadium, the deep-throated roars of jubilation were German, the flags which waved proudly in a victory salute were German . . . and they highlighted the bitterness of another Scottish defeat.

A defeat that meant Scotland were out of the World Cup. A defeat on a night of pageantry that was again the old story of failure for Scotland.

Yet . . . how different it might have been; for the sprinkling of Scots in the stadium could easily have been letting off the fireworks and ringing the bells for victory.

We had blue-shirted warriors spitting defiance, battling their brave hearts out on the vivid green grass, probably hitting back just too hard and revealing glimpses of fascinating football.

Scotland found one of the world's best attackers in Eddie Gray, of Leeds, and the team had a pattern and the men to give us a future, at least—if Brown could keep his team together.

Indeed, Scotland should have won the match for they played with heart, bite and resolution. But it was the Germans who went wild after their night of joy through strength and it was the Scots who cried tears of frustration.

It had been a night of tremendous drama, starting with a dream goal for Scotland and ending in humiliation with Celtic's Tommy Gemmell being ordered off for a foul on Haller.

It had also been a vicious game, always, in the electric atmosphere, on the verge of erupting into deadly violence.

Scotland started well, with the lithe, astute and fast Gray carving his name into Scottish football history with a brilliant move in the third minute.

His alert eye saw a gap and he calmly invaded German territory before unleashing a fierce shot which Maier in the home goal parried magnificently. But wee Jimmy Johnstone was on the spot to slip the ball into the net and Scotland had made the start we had prayed for.

SCARRED RECORD

For nearly half an hour the Scots were great, on top of the worried Germans, solid and reliable in defence and subtle and cool in the attack.

Then came one of the blunders which have so severely scarred our World Cup record. Billy McNeill passed back with Seeler threatening. Too speedy for Herriot, the ball went past for a corner. That brought the qualiser in 37 minutes, Fichtel being first to reach the ball and poke it into the net.

And disaster struck again in the second half.

As Beckenbauer was about to take a free-kick outside the Scottish penalty area, Muller seemed to push McNeill to the ground but the referee apparently didn't see the incident and Muller took the ball as it came into the penalty area and banged it into the net.

Once again gallant captain Bremner clapped his hands and roared his non-stop heroes in blue into attack. In 61 minutes justice was served. Alan Gilzean, who had been hampered, harried and kicked, was first to a high ball and, with a fine header, equalised.

Scotland looked World class at last, looked as though they were going to win their finest victory for the Germans were in retreat, stringing a thick white line across their goal as Scotland surged down on them, with Greig and Gemmell hammering into join the attack.

But the Germans had a subtle star in Stan Libuda. With 12 minutes to go, he took a long ball from Haller on the wing and spurted away. Gemmell challenged in vain. The winger ran on and ended a marvellous run with a shot which gave Herriot no chance.

Then came the ending the game could have well done without.

Fists were shaken at German players for too tough play and Scottish tempers boiled over. Some of the tackling was ferocious. The game was a tragedy for Gemmell, ordered off near the end for retaliating after a foul by Haller.

Afterwards, angry manager Bobby Brown lashed out and said Scotland had been kicked out of the World Cup and declared his players had been badly provoked and received little protection from the Swiss referee.

And he was irate because Haller, the man who had fouled Gemmell before the back retaliated, had escaped scot-free.

The teams were:

West Germany: Maier; Hottges, Vogts;

The man whose power was
missed against Germany—
John Hughes of Celtic

Beckenbauer, Schulz, Fichtel; Libuda, Seeler, Muller, Overath, Haller.

Scotland: Herriot; Greig, Gemmell; Bremner, McKinnon, McNeill; Johnstone, Gilzean, Stein, Gray, Cormack.

Referee: G. Droz, Switzerland.

So again Scotland's World Cup adventure had ended in disaster. We had beaten Cyprus twice, beaten Austria in Scotland, and drawn with Germany at home. The Hamburg defeat put us out and the one game to come, against Austria, did not matter. We lost it, anyhow.

And again we had to look to the future, to plan for success in the next World Cup.

Some said Scotland had been involved in too many rough matches and too many players had been in trouble with the referees and blamed our failure on a weakness in the

Out of luck is Alan Gilzean in a Scottish attack in one of the World Cup matches against West Germany

psychological side of the game—by being more flamboyant on the physical side.

For instance, it was claimed that Gemmell's indiscretion in Hamburg that had him ordered off was not by a long way the worst foul of the match. It just looked the worst and was good television because it was so open. It was also foolish.

Gemmell was punished later on—but others, especially in the German team, who had kicked and chopped and punched to greater effect, had gone their ways with characters unblemished.

Certainly it is known that Scottish players can be easily aroused and this brings trouble on them for they have often been provoked because the opposition knows it is worth while provoking them.

Anyhow, discipline in face of provocation is essential for Scottish players and if we are ever to win a World Cup we must have ball players to work with skill and keep the excitement low—and the physical out of it. Most of all, it is essential that our players learn to turn the other cheek.

Nevertheless, although it sounds a poor excuse, I have no doubt that Scotland has suffered more than most because of appalling refereeing.

Perhaps, however, the Scot's temperament is against him. The Scots are showy players in many ways, perhaps that little bit worse-tempered. They get into trouble because they hate to lose—and because of their heritage.

In the old days, when Scotland was even poorer than she is now, our young men of spirit became the world's most famous soldiers of fortune.

They fought with a dedication and toughness which sent shivers down the backs of enemies. Today our soccer stars are the modern equivalents. Their feet flash like rapiers—and, alas, too often so do their tongues. Especially when they are playing away from their native heath.

For they find that referees are not so strict as they are at home and when they see opponents calmly getting away with soccer mayhem they lose their rags. That's when the trouble starts. The Scot's ever-ready tongue lashes opponents who foul him—and referees who ignore his appeals. And the language difficulty is no barrier here for there's no mistaking the fury of the sounds of the angry Scot.

What Scots abroad in future must try to be, as well as splendid soldiers of fortune, are militant monks. Self-discipline is important.

But even more important, I insist, is keeping a good team intact for the next game—and the one after that—and the one after that.

Until we have a Scotland side playing like Celtic or Rangers or Leeds United, playing as a great club team, the players instinctively knowing what each other is going to do, we will never do well in the World Cup.

**Peter Cormack—the Hibs'
forward played well in Hamburg**

No Lack of Lions

Scotland still produce the brightest youngsters

THE Young Lions of Scotland are still roaring. Although this country—alas, as always!—failed to make a hit in the World Cup, there is no doubt that we are still the real home of outstanding footballers. And more and more clubs are pinning their faith in youthful talent.

Blunt, George Farm, Dunfermline Athletic manager who never pulls his punches, summed it up when he decided to stake the future of the famous Fife club on youngsters. He said: 'I'm sick of the so-called "experienced player" who gives only 100 per cent when he takes the notion. I am going to give youth a real chance. The kids are gluttons for work, they have talent and are loyal club men.'

Certainly, bright boys are again sprouting everywhere, just as they did in the golden past, on every factory pitch, miners' row and city street.

Sir Matt Busby, Manchester United's distinguished Scot, is another who feels this country's youngsters have no peers and he says: 'Scotland is the one country in the world where you don't need to have coaches to produce fine young players. Natural ball players seem to appear in a never-ending stream.'

Not everyone is pleased, however, at the current trend, which is to take boys straight from juvenile and amateur clubs to the senior grade and experienced Junior officials, for example, claim young players are not reaching their full potential because there is a vital gap in their schooling.

They are being made to miss the Junior grade and thus are being taken out of competitive football during their formative years.

Up to a point, I agree with this for I dispute allegations that Junior football is tough and unsophisticated, with the result that lads learn bad habits.

And I believe a young player cannot develop fully on the training ground or in reserve football, which is not really competitive. To my mind, the Junior grade hardens and sharpens a talent because it is competitive and because there is an exciting atmosphere about it, with the fans right down on top of the players. For there is more than sheer skill in football and the

Juniors add the extra something in competitiveness.

Perhaps this is where England score, perhaps this is why so many young Scots bloom so rapidly and brilliantly south of the border. Down south, lads miss the juniors, too—but there are really competitive leagues in which the colts can be blooded.

Not all Scottish clubs have turned against the Juniors, however. Celtic, for instance, have a lot of time for this grade of football and never refuse to help out any club or cause in this form of soccer. They also like their players to have Junior experience.

But the Juniors still flourish, with 180 clubs in membership, representing about 3,500 registered players. They must not be ignored.

Internal disputes about where lads should be played are, however, of minor importance when you consider what a vast reservoir of talent Scotland contains. Practically every club nowadays has youngsters of shining talent.

Now let's meet some of the Young Scottish Lions who are roaring lustily . . .

AT KILMARNOCK

A football 'party' and a study of an English star in action—these are the secrets of the success story of two up-and-coming Kilmarnock youngsters.

The 'party' was held at Rugby Park in a bid to sign Ross Mathie, whose goal-grabbing has made him a big favourite with the Kilmarnock supporters.

Gerry Queen had just been transferred from the Ayrshire club to Crystal Palace and the fans weren't too happy as they kept asking: 'Who's going to score the goals now?'

Manager Walter McCrae knew the man he needed—but it wasn't so easy to sign him. For although Ross Mathie had been highly recommended, manager McCrae

MacDonald—now isn't that a splendid name for young Scottish lions? On the left is 17-year-old Ian, who made his debut for Rangers on the left wing against Ayr United, and beside him is Alex, who stormed into top form for the Ibrox club last season

had been foiled every time he tried to get the lad on trial. For his team, Cambuslang Rangers, were still in the Junior Cup—they went on to win it that year—and naturally they were refusing to release any players on trial to senior clubs.

Walter McCrae, never short of an idea, solved his problem neatly—by inviting the whole Cambuslang team and officials down to Rugby Park for a midweek warm-up against his reserve side.

Everyone had a good time and before Mathie left the ground after the game he was on a provisional form for Kilmarnock.

Now he has become a first team regular, forming a fine striking partnership with Eddie Morrison and out-gunning even Gerry Queen in the goal-scoring department.

THE MIGHTY MITE

Another Kilmarnock player who hit the heights last season was that mighty mite, Jim Cook. The former Hearts' winger is just about the smallest player in senior football, only 63 inches tall. But Jim has a lion-heart in that small frame. And great ambition.

When he went to Blackpool on holiday not so long ago, he was down in the dumps. He had been freed by Hearts. He was not striking form at Rugby Park.

Then Jim watched a pre-season friendly. And that changed his life.

For playing in that match was Alan Ball. 'It was the first time I had seen the England player in action,' said Jim afterwards. 'But I thought he was terrific.'

So little Cook decided he would try to become a Ball of fire, too. After all, Ball is small like Cook. 'Yet,' added Jim, 'he could go for 90 minutes and never wasted a ball.'

That was the start of a new career for Cook. It wasn't all success, however. Jim

He's the youngest lion of them all—and one of the brightest. The name? Alec Morrison and although he is only 15 he has earned football fame, having played for Hamilton Acas' first team in the Scottish Cup

was so eager, so aggressive to get to the ball first he was booked.

Now, however, Walter McCrae has told him he has enough natural ability without worrying about niggling—and Jim Cook has been right on the ball.

AT DUNFERMLINE

One day, just a senior rookie—the next skipper of a renowned Scottish First Division team. That's the amazing story of 18-year-old Davie McNichol, of Dunfermline Athletic.

It must have been like a fairytale to young Dave, who had trained at Dundee for a year without getting a single game and was a first season senior at East End Park when manager George Farm told him he would captain the team against Celtic.

Farm, of course, had no worries. He said: 'I knew Dave would make it. I liked what I saw in him—clean cut, well-groomed, desperately eager.'

Anyhow, manager Farm had a skipper problem. When young McNicol was appointed club captain in January 1970, he was the ninth skipper the Fifers had seen in 18 months. This merry-go-round started when Roy Barry missed the opening of the season. Hugh Robertson deputised and then, in turn, Willie Callaghan, Bert Paton, Pat Gardner, Doug Baillie, Barrie Mitchell and Alex Edwards led the side.

McNicol is probably the youngest club captain in the history of the Scottish League but he revels in his job.

AT FIRHILL

Although Partick Thistle didn't enjoy a good season, there was one bright spot for the patient supporters of the Firhill club— the number of bright youngsters who made their mark.

Many of the Thistle young gallants have bright futures, none more likely to reach the heights than that fine winger, Bobby Lawrie, who was given a tough task—to take over from popular Arthur Duncan, who had been transferred to Hibernian.

Bobby, though, has made the Thistle fans forget all about Arthur with sparkling displays on the left wing. And just as happy as Arthur about the success story is a famous former Scottish international, Alex Parker once of Falkirk and Everton.

For 15 years ago Alex took Bobby in hand, putting him through the soccer hoop on a piece of waste ground in Irvine, Ayrshire.

When Alex was with Falkirk, he lived next door to Bobby's home and, although the new Thistle ace was only seven, the international began to coach him in the arts and crafts of the game.

When he grew up, Bobby Lawrie signed for Irvine Victoria while he was still at the local academy. Then he joined Portsmouth but they were forced to cut their staff and he was released.

The lad came home, was reinstated as a junior, then was signed, by Partick Thistle with Ayr United and Dundee United hot on his trail.

Bobby is a natural ball player with a golfing handicap of four and a cricket stroke that had Kilmarnock's Western Union club asking him to join.

But Bobby concentrates nowadays on football.

Nostalgic note:

In the Scottish Football Book for 1956-57, there was also a chapter about promising young Scottish players. Alex Parker was one of them. I wrote then: 'At 20, cheerful Alex Parker has probably the greatest future of any youngster in Scottish football. For already he is an international veteran and it looks as though he will be Scotland's right-back for years to come.'

How time flies.

AT FIR PARK

Does it pay to be versatile? That's always been the cause of hot arguments in football. Undoubtedly managers feel that a lad who can, with distinction, play in many positions is a great fellow to have around. But is it fair to the player to continue to field him one day as a forward, the next as a defender?

Frankly, few top stars have gained their illustrous places in soccer's hall of fame because of their versatility.

Sammy Cox, of Rangers, was one of the games greats and he starred in many positions. So did Andy Kerr, of Partick Thistle and Kilmarnock, who was capped at back for Scotland and gained most of his cheers as an unorthodox centre-forward. But these two were exceptions and it is usually a wise course for an up-and-coming laddie to try to make one position his own.

That's the view of Motherwell's Keith MacRae, an apprentice journalist and certainly one of the handiest players any club ever had around, a young man who can make a real name for himself in practically any berth. But Keith has decided his right position is goalkeeper. He had been invited by Motherwell manager Bobby Howitt, who feels young players no matter

Motherwell's Brian Heron is a young man with a future, although he had an in-and-out time of it last season at Ibrox, starting as a reserve winger, playing in the first team at full-back and then returning to the second team. But he is a lad with talent

Versatile Keith MacRae, of Motherwell, can star in many positions. But he wants most to become a Scotland goalkeeper and he is getting his chance in the Motherwell goal

how versatile should concentrate on one role, to choose a permanent place at Fir Park. Keith felt he should stick to the sweater.

And there can be little doubt that the well-built youngster with the flame-coloured hair will be a great Scotland keeper of the future. Last season, for instance, he held his first team place in opposition to league international Peter McCloy.

He was included in the pool for the Under-23 Scotland team—and that nailed any doubt Keith had about himself, endorsing his decision to forget about becoming a great wing-half or full-back—or even centre-forward. He had been a hit in all those positions and had even been the reserve side's leading scorer.

But from now on it's goalkeeping for Keith MacRae—unless, of course, in an emergency.

AT THE READY

In Scotland, too, are even younger players, bright teenagers on the verge of the big breakthrough to real glory.

And one of the most impressive debuts was made on 17 January 1970, by Rangers' 17-year-old winger, Ian MacDonald, who scored a goal against Ayr United and made a tremendous contribution to the game. Ian, fresh-faced, modest, had been only five months at Ibrox when he made his spectacular first appearance. No wonder manager Willie Waddell said: 'I'm delighted with Ian.'

The lad from an Edinburgh juvenile team looks every inch an international winger of the future, with deft footwork, speed and a big heart. He used to be a Hearts fan—but not any more. Like so many other lads from the East who became heroes of Ibrox, young Ian is Rangers-daft now.

Keep an eye, too, on Neil Murray of Hearts, a forward whom Tynecastle mana-

They're small—but they have yards and yards and yards of real football talent. They're Kilmarnock's wingers Jim Cook and Tommy McLean

ger Johnny Harvey feels is right in the mould of the old-time masters of the craft.

Murray is an M.A., a graduate of Aberdeen University—but for the time being he is a full-time footballer. That was the second gamble Neil took last season.

He wasn't sure whether he should join Hearts at all for he was happy playing for Ross County, Hearts fans are happy that he decided to go to Edinburgh. He can be a new Tommy Walker.

Celtic have, perhaps, the most flourishing crop of bright youngsters in Scotland. And Sir Robert Kelly, the club chairman who has always felt youth should play a great part in football, feels the Parkhead kids will soon provide the fans with a team even better than the great side who won the European Cup in Lisbon.

'I think there is a greater wealth of raw material in the young players at Parkhead today than when our present first team began to take shape,' said Sir Robert.

'We are, of course, very pleased about it for the great sides of the past, such as Spurs, Manchester United, Hungary and even Brazil, had a few years of glory, then slipped because they did not have the same talent coming up through the ranks. We made sure that didn't happen to us.'

And when you look at the names of some of the bright boys who are making Celtic reserves almost as big an attraction as the top team, you gaze at the names of Scotland players in the making.

David Hay has broken through. Lou Macari has impressed in his first team outings. And there more, such as Vic Davidson and Ken Dalglish who will make sure there is no chance of the Celtic bubble bursting for a long time to come.

Here's the winger all Perth feels should be in the Scotland team—the able Kenny Aird, of St. Johnstone ▶

IT'S THAT TOUGH QUIZ AGAIN

Are you really a superior fan? Can you argue with the best referees about the rules—and be proved right? Do you know your soccer history? Are you well-informed about football lore? Are you, in short, an expert on our great game?

You are? Good. Here's a chance to show your skill—in our famous not-so-easy quiz.

1—It's half time and you, the referee, are enjoying a well-earned cup of tea in the dressing room. But next door one of the players isn't happy. He isn't happy about you—and he is telling all his mates just what an idiot of a referee you are. He is criticising all your decisions, your approach to the game, your dress, your looks and your parentage. He is saying all this in a loud voice and in the bluest of language. You cannot help but over-hear. So you go into the players' dressing-room and tell Mr. Loudmouth that he cannot play in the second half. You have ordered him off.

Have you made the correct decision?

2—Now—a few teasers. On which ground in England have Scottish Cup-ties been played? What are the dimensions of the penalty area? Put the following clubs in order of seniority—Celtic, Aberdeen, Kilmarnock, Stranraer, Hibernian, Rangers. Which club won the Scottish Cup while in the Second Division—and when?

3—A wing-half is about to take a throw-in. Up comes an opponent and stands a couple of yards away. The referee blows his whistle—and orders the player to stand 10 yards away. Was the ref right?

4—Nowadays nicknames don't seem to be as popular as they used to be. But some are still in use. So—who are (a) The Cobblers, (b) The Hammers, (c) The Canaries, (d) The Lambs, (e) The Pilgrims, (f) The Ironsides, (g) The Stags, (h) The Brewers? Well, I told you it wasn't an easy quiz.

5—What was peculiar about the appearance of the famous Alec Raisbeck, one of Scotland's greatest centre-halves, when he played football in the early 1900s?

6—When was the Scottish Football Association formed? When was the Scottish League started? Who were the first champions of the Scottish League?

7—In season 1955–56, Accrington Stanley set up a record in England which has never been equalled. It is a record with a real tartan flavour. What was it?

8—Why are the following dates historic? 1924. 1893. 1891–92.

9—Charles II was known as the Merry Monarch. But—do you know why he is mentioned in football history?

If you can answer all these, you get the award of Scotland's most knowledgeable football fan.

And you deserve it . . .

Answers

1—Yes. There can be argument, of course, about this one. But if the remarks were made in a loud voice the referee is entitled to take action—just as he could if this happens on the field. However, if the player was talking normally to his colleagues the referee wasn't entitled to listen in—for that would be eavesdropping.

2—Shielfield Park, home of Berwick Rangers. 44 yds. × 18 yds. Kilmarnock (born 1869), Stranraer (1870), Rangers (1873), Hibs (1875), Celtic (1887), Aberdeen (1903). East Fife won the Scottish Cup in 1938 while in the Second Division.

3—The referee was wrong. Although at a free-kick, the opposing players must be 10 yds. distant, this doesn't apply at a throw-in.

4—(a) Cobblers—Northampton, (b)— Hammers—West Ham, (c) Canaries— Norwich, (d) Lambs—Notts County (e) Pilgrims—Plymouth Argyle, (f) Ironsides —Middlesbrough and Newport, (g) Stags —Mansfield Town, (h) Brewers—Watford.

5—Alec Raisbeck was one of the few outfield players in football to wear spectacles.

6—The S.F.A. were formed in 1873, the Scottish League in 1890. First champions were Dumbarton and Rangers with 29 points each.

7—Accrington Stanley set up a record in 1955–56 by fielding a side which included all Scottish-born players. Their all-Scottish side made several appearances in the Third Division North during the season. In fact, all but four of the 19 players who appeared for Stanley during 1955–56 were born in Scotland.

8—1924—it was decided that a goal could be scored direct from a corner kick. 1893— professionalism was legalised in Scotland. 1891–92—penalty kick was introduced.

9—Charles II was the first king to show favour towards football, a game which up till his time had been bitterly condemned by rulers. Charles patronised a game between his servants and those of the Duke of Abermarle in 1681.

Your score . . . . . .

What a great goal!

Like this one. It is a goal from a daring header by one of Scotland's princes of goal-grabbers, Colin Stein, of Rangers. The centre-forward scored it against Kilmarnock at Ibrox and it was one of the most spectacular of the season.

And these are the men the fans love most, the goal-scorers. For goals are what football is really about. The more goals the better the entertainment, the more the spectators love the game. Thank goodness in Scotland we still have the chance to cheer grand and glorious goals.

These goals captured by our photographers had the crowds roaring last season.

It happens in a flash. One second and there seems to the defenders to be no danger; the next, they are appalled as an attacker, his timing perfect, his courage medal-worthy and his skill uncanny, swoops to score a brilliant goal.

Impossible to score from this angle? You might think so—but not if agile Davie Robb is around. The Aberdeen forward never gives up, considers goals can be scored from all angles and distances. That's why he is one of our bright young attackers. In this picture, (below) Robb has the Airdrie defenders bewildered as he scores when no goal seemed on

'Feed the Bear' chant the overjoyed Celtic supporters when John 'Yogi' Hughes storms into action. And the big forward has scored some of Scotland's most dramatic goals. Here (above) you see one of his most valuable, if not one of his best . . . the winning goal against Hibernian at Easter Road

You can't see his head but he's there all right, Willie Johnston, of Rangers, that brilliant attacker who moves so slickly and strikes so venomously. There is class in all his moves and poor Partick Thistle defenders know that as the Ranger scores a fine goal

It isn't all that often the Celtic defenders are in trouble. But they are here (*above*). And you realise it must be a fine move to beat them. This was. It was one designed by the clever St. Johnstone in one of their glory days at Parkhead. The scorer: Fred Aitken, the up-and-coming Muirton winger

The only consolation for the 'keeper here (*below*) is that he had absolutely no chance as Ayr United's Jackie Ferguson hammered the ball high into the net

Now, here's a goal to remember, a goal stamped with class and skill and agility. Willie Wallace, of Celtic (*above*) is scoring against Airdrie. It was a work of art, a poem of a goal. For Wallace took a difficult pass with the aplomb of a Di Stefano, killed the ball, then smashed it into the net

Well, no doubt about what happened here (*below*). The ball's in the back of the net—the Celtic net. Dropping to the ground in disgust is Jim Brogan after a blunder. Goalkeeper Williams sits and sighs. But Dunfermline's Gillespie runs back in delight after scoring at Parkhead

It can be dangerous to score. But it's worth it. And Rangers' Alex McDonald is smothered in congratulations by overjoyed colleagues after scoring against Hibernian at Ibrox

Hibs are on the receiving end in this picture (*below*). Scorer this time is Celtic's Jimmy Johnstone

FAREWELL TO THE SIXTIES

A decade dazzling or ...?

He helped make the sixties swing—Rangers dazzling winger, Willie Henderson

I T was one of the most dramatic decades in sport—the ten years from 1960 until 1970. It threw up more than a fair share of heroes. In football, we had Pele, Best, Johnstone, Baxter, Eusebio, Charlton.

Now that it's over, will we look back on it as a Dazzling Decade? Were they the Sizzling Sixties, the Scintillating Sixties.

Certainly they should have been—for never had a football decade begun with such style, drama and brilliantly natural intepretation of the game.

At Hampden, the world's most historic ground, Real Madrid and Eintracht of Germany had a vast crowd of 127,261

entranced with the most fascinating football exhibition Scotland, or, for that matter, any other country, had ever seen.

It was 18 May 1960, and Real won the European Cup final by 7–3 and we all believed a new era in football had started—an era of glittering ball skills, fluid movement, exhilarating attacking play, an era, in short, of the gay football so beloved of the Scots.

Did we get it?

Will the Sixties go down in soccer history as the star-dusted decade? These questions still dangle curiously.

Well, we got Celtic. To their eternal credit and everlasting fame, Celtic brought Scotland her greatest footballing glory by becoming the first British club to win the European Cup.

They did it by beating Inter-Milan in Lisbon in 1967—seven years after Real had enchanted us—and with an exhibition of football that was also laced with magic.

More, Celtic set a standard.

Celtic gave Europe, so long hag-ridden by grim, negative defensive tactics, a real—yes, Real or Royal, if you like—conception of the most glorious game in the world—method plus magic; the magic of exhilarating attack.

So, as the Seventies set in, Celtic are still the club on top, still the club most lovers of football all over the world like to watch.

Celtic, indeed, were the club who, with Manchester United, also lovers of the free expression of the polished footballer, did most in Britain to make the Sixties memorable.

Alas, the Sixties contained more frustration than exhilaration.

There was the Scotland international team. In 1960, on a golden October day at Belfast's Windsor Park, it seemed that the men in blue were going to emulate Real Madrid.

Scotland beat Ireland 4–0. We had put the accent on youth and the boys gave a delightful exhibition of controlled football.

The reports were ecstatic. No reason to doubt that this young eleven could keep it up and lads such as John White and Denis Law had shown the touches of real greatness.

I wrote that at the time. And—'What was pleasing, too, was the planning which had gone into our tactics. Moves had been well rehearsed. The future seems bright.'

Team manager? Andy Beattie, who had been boss before and was to be only first of the many managers Scotland had in the Sixties.

Remember the team that was to give Scotland new pride in her international adventuring? Brown (Spurs); Caldow (Rangers), Hewie (Charlton); Evans (Celtic), Mackay (Spurs), McCann (Motherwell); Leggatt (Fulham), White (Falkirk), St. John (Motherwell), Law (Huddersfield), Mulhall (Aberdeen).

What happened after that?

We played England on a sunny, windy day in April—full of hope. When weren't we hopeful?

But things had gone wrong. Spurs couldn't release Brown, Mackay and White, who had joined them from Falkirk. Brown's

**Jimmy Johnstone, of Celtic . . .
Is he the greatest winger of
them all?**

deputy, George Niven, of Rangers, was hurt and the third goalkeeping substitute, Frank Haffey, of Celtic, took over.

On the Wednesday before the international Rangers and Celtic met at Hampden in a Scottish Cup semi-final replay.

There was no Belfast form. Scotland drew 1—1 with England. But it was a poor game.

Even worse, the standard for what was to be Scotland's performances in the decade was set.

Worries about Anglos being released, injuries, lack of consistency, failure to field the same eleven time after time, changes at the top with one team manager following another—was it any wonder that at World Cup level we became the joke of the rest of the footballing nations?

Up and down . . . breathing hot, then cold. That was poor old Scotland. For a spell Wembley became a nightmare, with England slaughtering us in 1961 by 9–3. The World Cup became even worse.

We failed to qualify in the Sixties and the real reason wasn't hard to find. Dreadful inconsistency. Season 1961–62 was the perfect—or dreadful—example.

The horror of Wembley was forgotten and, in September, the Hampden Roar was re-born as we seemed again to have found a team of skill and spirit, giving us hope for the future as well as a World Cup 3–2 victory over powerful Czechoslovakia.

Friendly rivals . . . Ronnie McKinnon, of Rangers, and Celtic's Billy McNeill (right) leave the S.F.A. headquarters in Glasgow together after the famous 'talk-in' on the troubles at 'Old Firm' games

At wing-half, Scotland had discovered the fine partnership of Pat Crerand and Jim Baxter. We had Denis Law at his best, Law with all the flamboyance of a big brass band, Law the genius with the jerky, jazzy action.

And then? Same old story. We failed to qualify for the World Cup finals. Because? The same old story. Injuries, failure to get the stars, changes.

But Scotland was always a Phoenix in the Sixties, a Phoenix rising with bagpipes blowing and claymores flashing from the ashes of defeat and humiliation.

In April, it was soccer slaughter in the Hampden sun—but this time Scotland were the killers, England the slaughtered. Another great Scottish team, the Hampden Wizards we called them, gave England a football lesson with a performance that should have been accompanied throughout by a roll of drums and a commentary by Olivier. Scotland won 2–0 after a quarter of a century of Hampden failure.

So we became a great international side at last?

Alas, no.

A month later the Scots lost 3–2 to Uruguay—at Hampden.

Need I say more?

The international story hasn't changed. The decade finished with Scotland losing once again in the World Cup to Germany and Austria.

Up and down, up and down—Scotland's international serial is a liftman's nightmare. Nearly there . . . there . . . then—slump to defeat once again. Horror Wembleys. . . . Happy Wembleys—that was our lot in the Sixties.

What stands out most, I repeat, is: Lack of consistency.

Malcolm Muggeridge has said the Sixties were a frenetic decade, having, however, more the character of a foolish dream than a nightmare.

So it was in football.

And there was nothing more foolish, to my mind, than the new method play which made its dubious presence felt in the Sixties. It made the Sixties a rugged decade.

For it was the decade of the robots, the faceless ones. The hired assassin in football made his debut, the player whose main job was to see opposing stars were kept quiet.

It worked. England became the first country to win the World Cup with a team of dour efficiency which made those who had loved Matthews and Finney and Lawton shudder.

Many other teams copied the style. Functional football became the thing. It brought success. No doubt about that. But it was really a foolish dream. For the average fan didn't like it. He preferred joy in his game. He loved the virtuoso player. He hated to see his favourite artists clobbered.

And as we march into the Seventies it is pleasing to see that dull method, the craze for the Cattenachio, is on the way out.

This is Santamaria, the once famous centre-half of Real Madrid, who ushered in the sixties in such great style at Hampden

There is, of course, more method than ever at the back. But attackers are again being allowed more freedom of expression—by England, by Leeds, by nearly all the other clubs who took entertainment out of football in the hunt for success and who are now trying to make soccer fluid again.

Yet, despite the move in the mid-sixties to machine-like football, nothing could stop the exuberant player, the richly-gifted extrovert, coming to the fore.

Some of the thrill came from glorious shooting—by full-backs. Tommy Gemmell, of Celtic, was one, and this buccaneering

These great Scots made the sixties sizzle—Willie Johnston, Jimmy Johnstone, Willie Wallace , Dennis Law, team manager John Prentice and Billy Bremner

defender was the toast of Scotland with many wonderful goals, none of which bettered his score in the European Cup-tie against Benfica at Parkhead as the decade was ending.

Not only in Scotland did the fans see the solo artist in all his glory.

ADORING FANS

Pele of Brazil reached his peak. So did Eusebio of Portugal. Colour meant nothing in football, no matter the problems in other fields. And these were tremendous players who could command thousands of pounds in salary—and even more thousands of adoring fans.

In England, George Best was the player of the age. He had the glamour of a Beatle, the money sense of a Clore. But his football was brilliant, ageless. He was Irish, of course. And great Scots gave flavour to practically every English club.

But England, too, were producing fine players—a maturing Alan Ball, a sprightly Francis Lee, and a formidable squad of goalkeepers extraordinary, including Banks and Bonetti.

The Sixties saw a famine in Scottish goalkeepers, though in other positions we had supurb exponents, the late John White, Jim Baxter, Willie Henderson, Denis Law, Mackay, Wilson.

Most colourful, most popular when in the mood: Celtic's Jimmy Johnstone, per-

haps to be in the Seventies the greatest winger of them all.

New names will make the headlines in the Seventies. There's no question of that. But there is doubt as to whether a strong challenge will be mounted to Celtic and Rangers, now Waddell-managed and orientated for success.

The Sixties may not have been as dazzling as we might have wished but they showed that the old lion could roar, in football, at least, even if most of the home play did not bring the sensation of the Pill, Lady Chatterley's Lover, the Rolling Stones or a visit to the moon.

But we had many records in football in the Sixties—Britain's biggest crowd for a floodlit match, the 107,500 who saw the Scotland–Poland World Cup-tie at Hampden in 1965 and were, of course disappointed . . . transfers topped £100,000, the first being the £116,000 paid by Manchester United to Turin for Denis Law in 1962.

We had close-circuit television, the World Cup was stolen from an exhibition in London and recovered by a dog named Pickles, Rangers had three different managers, Symon, White and Waddell, in just over two years and substitutes became a new part of the game.

We had violence on the terracings, the demise of Third Lanark, the invasion of talent from Scandinavia, and Sir Stanley Matthews became football's first knight.

One of the great moments of the sixties—the Scottish team, including Davy Wilson, Willie Henderson and John White celebrate a great win over England at Wembley

All human life is there...
...on the football pitch

No doubt about it. You get more than a game of football when you hand your money over at the turnstile. You get ... well, you get practically everything. As that popular Sunday newspaper says of itself modestly: All human life is here ...

It is true, of course, that sometimes we feel not only humans are present at football matches; for we have told referees, for instance, that their decisions are out of this world, watched in disgust conduct on the terracings that is anything but civilised and shuddered at tackles more suited to the jungle than an ordered sport of the seventies.

On the whole, however, football remains a pleasant spectacle. And more. It is a kaleidoscope of life. Humour, excitement, drama, emotion, histrionics, tragedy—all can be packed into the 90 minutes of a soccer match.

Yes, the football pitch is a stage. Take your choice ... Striptease or ballet? ... Conflict or commiseration? These pictures vividly portray life, grave and gay, violent and humorous, in the world of football. ...

Striptease?

There's a laugh from the crowd as Willie Johnston, of Rangers, blushingly dons a new pair of pants after his original pair were torn in a match against Raith Rovers at Kirkaldy

Ballet ?

It looks so graceful at Ibrox as Davie Provan, Harry Hood, Jim Brogan, and Sandy Jardine are caught in a classic pose. But it's really a tough tussle for the ball in a Rangers-Celtic match which can never be said to have the atmosphere of a ballet

Elation

Smiles spread on the faces of Celtic players Craig, Hay, Chalmers, Callaghan, Hughes and Auld after the goal scored by Auld in the League Cup Final against St. Johnstone—the goal which won

Dejection

Disappointment is written over the faces of
St. Johnstone manager Willie Ormond and
Gordon Whitelaw as they leave the Hampden
pitch after losing to Celtic in the League Cup
Final

Iron Curtain

Ayr United spread a curtain of defenders around Rangers' Colin Stein in a game at Somerset Park.

Mystery

The goal gapes wide—but the ball doesn't go into the net. It flies over the bar—and Celtic players wonder just how that happened, with St. Johnstone defenders spreadeagled on the

Hold-up?

Hey, let's go . . . that seems to be the cry of Rangers' Jim Baxter as Raith Rovers' Millar is telling him: 'Don't go, Jim!' The man behind Millar is Rangers' Johnston

Conflict

Kilmarnock's Frank Beattie tries to calm the uproar after tempers rise in a Fairs Cities Cup-tie between the Rugby Park club and Bacau of

Contact !

Playing footsie are Kai Jahansen, of Rangers, and Raith Rovers' Sinclair

Commiseration

Oh, the agony of it all! And Hibernian's Jonny Graham stoops to comfort injured colleague, Arthur Duncan in a game at Ibrox

Anticipation

All the tension, all the alertness of football is shown here as Dunfermline defenders and Celtic forward John Hughes get ready for a corner kick

The age of soccer violence? Perhaps. But, in Scotland, the name of the game is still—entertainment

Is this the age of violence in football? Is the great game becoming dirtier? Is money playing too big a part? Is the real joy departing because of ruthless professionalism and relentless insistence on system play?

Thousands upon thousands of words have been spoken and written recently about football, still the world's most popular sport, and most of them have been pessimistic, most of them asserting that football has lost its soul, that anything goes, that the game is destroying itself.

Here are just a few examples:

'The game is getting terrible. You used to go out on the field and enjoy yourself—you don't any more. The skill factor is being wrung out of the game'—Pat Crerand, former Scottish international.

'The game reflects our times—the age of dissension'—Alan Hardacre, secretary of the English Football League.

'Everyone expects an answer to violence in football from the referees. But we can't do much. Often we make things worse by sending a player off and then the situation becomes more tense. The solution lies with the directors, the managers, the public, the Press'—Istvan Zsolt, of Hungary, one of the world's best-known referees.

There is no doubt that violence is on the increase in England and one of the biggest troubles as football becomes more global is the disparity between the European and the Latin American concept of the rules.

Indeed, Estudiantes players were jailed for their dreadful onslaughts on AC Milan players in Beunos Aires in the World Club championship.

But what about Scotland? Is the violence rate soaring here, too? Has the time come to call a halt?

I say No. Certainly the game in this country has become more physical. There is also more accent now on method play. And there has crept into our game an insidious practice from abroad—the feigning of injury, the practice of going down after a tackle as if mortally wounded in the hope that an opponent will be penalised.

Of course, there are hard men in the Scottish game. There always have been. But I believe sincerely that the average Scottish player loves the game, loves to play it, wants to win by sheer skill rather than by shady tactics, scorns consistently foul play and try to express his talents in a free and natural way.

As always, however, the referees are being blamed for what is said to be an increase in the crime rate in Scotland. Have our referees gone back? Should they become full-time professionals?

I maintain that Scottish referees are still the best in the world. If they have a weakness it is that too many see only the refereeing part of the game. As English star referee

Gordon has put it so ably: A referee's role
should be to help the players and the public
get more enjoyment from the match.
Referees should not make a deliberate effort
to control but to take part. Too few recog-
nise the players' love of the game.

In other words, too many referees think
only of themselves in a schoolmaster's role,
think they must dictate and control.

It is difficult, however, for any referee to
stamp out gamesmanship.

There is no doubt that many players
feign injury to upset their opponents'
rhythm. But what can the referee do? He

daren't take the risk of playing on after someone falls to the ground. It could be a broken leg.

However, as method suffocates so many footballing countries, with physical effort the main aim and 'sheer professionalism' covering sins which would have brought blushes of shame only a few years ago, Scotland still produces distinguished artists, individualists of the highest skills, Jimmy Johnstone, Tommy McLean, Peter Marinello, Willie Henderson, John Connelly, Jim Blair. . . .

Skill is not yet strangled in Scotland, even though technique today has advanced to include those in the split-second category —the ability to control a hard-driven ball, to lay off a pass first time. Scottish stars could always baffle opponents and even in these days of tight marking they can make space for themselves . . . the modern stamp of genius.

NOT APPEALING

Not everyone, however, is convinced football is all it should be in Scotland. One man who thinks system football isn't appealing and that too much of it is being played here is Hearts manager John Harvey, who says:

'I don't like system football, although like others we have had to play it at Tynecastle for we had to conform while we were rebuilding. Like the others we have sometimes had to put results first.

'But I do not like it. Often I feel we are in danger of killing our national talent. Sometimes boys of real talent can no longer find a place because they cannot fit a pattern while others of mediocre talent are hailed as stars. I think it's all wrong.'

I agree here. That's the touble with method football. It kills the individualist, the boy of real talent.

The type of artistic player Scots like—Alex Willoughby, of Aberdeen

All-time Scottish great, Bobby Collins, who came back to his own country to join Morton. His was always great Scottish style play

Whether or not John's remedy would suit, however, I don't know. He says that, in this age of fear, with the threat of relegation so terrible, promotion and relegation should stop for a couple of years.

'If they did that,' he added, 'the football would be fantastic. People would be surprised at how natural and beautiful it would become. We could be back as leaders in modern football.'

PROGRESS?

That's a tempting thought but there is no doubt that the result is beginning to matter just as much here in Scotland as it does in England and that results mean more than attractive football in many cases.

Of this aspect, the respected Spurs manager Bill Nicholson, so well known north of the border, has this to say: 'Because of the money involved, it is necessary to get results these days and it affects managers, directors, players. You can use the word professionalism, you can call it progress. Progress it's supposed to be but progress in which direction? How important is winning, really, when it's giving football a bad name?'

CORRUPTION?

Nevertheless, football continues to be, on the whole, entertaining in Scotland. Much more so, if I may say so, than it is in England where I'm convinced winning the World Cup the way England did has had a corrupting influence.

Many of my newspaper friends in England think the same way now. They were, of course, happy that England did win the premier trophy. Now, though, they are realising there was a price—and the price was the sacrifice of football with a

Another brilliant Scottish player—Andy Penman, of Rangers

flair, football with a polish and a verve, football with a brilliant style to the faceless football of the method men.

For clubs copied the winning style.

But while elegant football has gone out of fashion in the south, while it has become more violent, perhaps the England team, the team who won the World Cup, can lead a renaissance for I have seen signs recently that they can play football that is attractive as well as effective.

POETRY AND MUSIC

In Scotland I feel method will never take over completely. The Scot loves football too much for that to happen. Football is in his blood; it is a way of self-expression. And to the Scot football is poetry, music, art; football must be beautiful, sweet, lovingly performed.

As always, players in Scotland are allowed to express themselves. And the lead comes from the most successful Scottish team of this decade, Celtic, whose manager, Jock Stein, never curbs the individual talent of his stars, although there is a modern framework of method.

But Celtic have welded the old and the new and made an even more attractive style. Other clubs are trying to follow. Scotland not only has players of great talent, she has bright young managers trying to guide them.

Despite the moans from other countries, despite the disturbing increase in violence, the state of the game in Scotland is healthy.

Sheer artistry—that's what Scottish fans love. And here's Jim Baxter of Rangers providing it

The gallant Saints . . . but Celtic take the League Cup

A T last, football fever was burning in the Fair City of Perth. It had taken a long time to develop. Not that Perth wasn't interested in football. It was. But although St. Johnstone had been playing since 1884 this was the first year the club had stormed into football's big-time, the final of a national tournament. And the citizens of the douce town were behind their team to a man, confident that St. Johnstone could win the Scottish League Cup Final of 1969.

There had been exciting times at Muirton that autumn, the most thrilling the Perth enthusiasts had ever known—thanks mainly to a smiling, round-faced football expert called Willie Ormond, once a member of the Famous Five Hibernian forward line and a Scottish international left-winger and now a manager of distinction.

Willie had made football flourish in Perth, and that wasn't easy; for Perth didn't really expect top footballing honours to come to their placid city.

There had always been an easy-going air about St. Johnstone, worthy opponents for the best but never expected to land trophies and titles.

Perhaps it was the club's setting. Muirton is one of the most picturesque grounds in Scotland and from the stand one could take in the glorious view of the splendid Perthshire hills and glowing countryside.

Perhaps it was the lack of atmosphere.

In Perth was none of the bustle and hustle and exciting rustle of the big soccer crowds, none of the high pressure liveliness which marks football in Glasgow and the industrial west of Scotland.

Perth enjoyed football in a quiet way. But few of the enthusiasts expected their club to reach Hampden in a cup final or win the league championship. After all, the first big event in St. Johnstone's history had been the winning of the Consolation Cup in 1913–14 and, to be frank, precious little more in the way of honours had ever been gained by Saints.

It's true they won admission to the Second Division in 1921. It's true they won the championship of that division in 1924. It's true they have gone through to the semi-final of the Scottish Cup. And it's true that they once finished fifth in the First Division table.

But the best the fans hoped for was that St. Johnstone would keep a place in the First Division. 'Sturdy provincials'—that was the St. Johnstone tag through the years. To be fair, it was the correct appellation.

And then came Ormond and a new

sprouting of football enthusiasm in Perth.

Things were really buzzing in Perth in the autumn of 1969. St. Johnstone were the talk of the football world—a first-class professional team, offering a real challenge to the giants of the First Division.

They had scored eight goals at Firhill against Partick Thistle, the most they had ever scored against First Division opposition, and they were playing with method, sense, flair; playing, too, attractive football that had the neutrals flocking to watch them.

One of the reasons for their success was that Willie Ormond had come to terms with the difficulties of running a provincial club in Scotland. He had, he explained simply, to 'play for the day'. There was no point, he added, in instituting a youth policy and looking years ahead; for little clubs like St.

Champagne Celts—and no wonder the Parkhead aces are singing in their baths at Hampden. They have just won the Scottish League Cup—for the fifth time. They also set up a record that may never be equalled. It was the fourth time Celtic had won a major trophy in six months. On 5 April 1969, they beat Hibs in the postponed League Cup Final; on 22 April they collected the League Championship when Rangers lost to Dundee; on 26 April they beat Rangers in the Scottish Cup Final. And when this picture was taken on 25 October they had just beaten St. Johnstone in the 1969 League Cup Final

The goal that gave Celtic
their record. Bertie Auld scores
coolly at Hampden

Johnstone would have great difficulty in keeping good young players.

His policy was: 'Try to keep the team winning and then introduce a young player. But boys win nothing in this game. More than ever, it is experience that counts.'

Willie Ormond was chock-full of ideas. One was to 'hammer' his players as hard as possible on their first training session after a match, a reversal of normal procedure. In that way, the manager felt, after-the-match stiffness was eased more quickly.

There was talk, too, that Ormond had based his style on that of the Famous Five—Smith, Johnstone, Reilly, Turnbull and Ormond—of Hibernian, with cute switching of positions the key.

Said Willie: 'I agree our attacks look

good at times, perhaps reminiscent of those raids we used at Easter Road. But I don't rehearse these moves. The forwards have virtually a free hand to play it off the cuff.

'It is simply a case of using the ball as well as working off it.'

There was no doubt, however, that great thought had gone into the St. Johnstone technique. Ormond and trainer Frank Christie were never off the field during the week, planning free-kicks, corner-kicks and throw-ins.

Perhaps the real secret was that Willie Ormond, although he had players of rare talent in the likes of John Connelly, Henry Hall and Kenny Aird, had found lads who were 'Indians and not chiefs'.

'They are all workers,' said Ormond, 'and I have always believed that the way to blend players is to have strength and skill in the right places.'

So he had little Henry Hall in front and big Buck McCarry behind him, for example. 'I try to have a little player covered by a big fellow,' he went on, 'and a clever player balanced by a strong one, then it all falls into a pattern without putting numbers to it. The only way is to have the pattern developing from the blend. I would never set out the pattern first in numbers and then bend the players to fit it.'

That was the football policy, the philosophy and the sincere belief of manager Willie Ormond in the autumn of 1969.

And it was bringing glowing success, success they had never dreamed of, to Muirton.

The quality of the work was showing in

And this is how it feels to score at Hampden. Auld holds his arm high in delight

Celtic captain Billy McNeill (*right*) goes near with a header against St. Johnstone in the League Cup Final

the fast feet of the St. Johnstone players for no team in Scotland was quicker to the ball.

Ormond gave the credit to his players but his own shrewdness could not be overlooked. He had, for instance, transferred Alex MacDonald to Rangers for £50,000 and bought, for £15,000, the neat Henry Hall, from Stirling Albion. Hall's nippiness was just what St. Johnstone needed. Also making a name for himself was 19-year-old John Connelly, a young inside-forward with a smooth style and a fierce shot.

So Perth was becoming known for the quality of its football rather than its famous whisky.

Football fame had been at last achieved.

But now Willie Ormond's St. Johnstone faced the most worrying task in the club's history.

They had won through for the first time to the final of a national competition, the League Cup.

But their opponents were—Celtic.

Celtic were determined, that 25 October 1969, to win the League Cup for the fifth year running. And they started favourites.

But it seemed that most of the inhabitants of Perth had come to Hampden, convinced that their sparkling team would win their first big honour.

A crowd of 73,067 turned out at Hampden to watch—and that was a notable tribute to the prowess of the fighting Saints.

There was a sensation before the start. Celtic showed the faith they had in their vast pool of players by leaving out World Cup back, Tommy Gemmell, who had been ordered off in the West Germany–Scotland match in Hamburg just before the League Cup final, and making another World Cup star, Jimmy Johnstone, their 12th man.

This was the line-up:

Celtic: Fallon; Craig, Hay; Murdoch, McNeill, Brogan; Callaghan, Hood, Hughes, Chalmers, Auld. *Sub:* Johnstone.

St. Johnstone: Donaldson; Lambie, Coburn; Gordon, Rooney, McPhee; Aird, Hall, McCarry, Connolly, Aitken. *Sub:* Whitelaw.

Referee: J. Paterson, Bothwell.

Alas for the Saints. Cup Final nerves seemed to hit them and before they had become used to the vast acres of the stadium those regulars of Hampden, Celtic, had shattered them with such devastating raids that they could have been three goals down in the first five minutes.

Indeed, it was a fantastic start. In the first minute, St. Johnstone's hopes were high as Fred Aitken carved a fine opening and Henry Hall was on the spot—only to mistime his shot. Then—away raced Celtic.

John Hughes cut through, beat Rooney, crossed accurately. Chalmers's header flew

Another near thing for Saints as John Hughes, of Celtic, puts the ball just past the post

netwards. Big 'keeper Donaldson parried the ball on to the bar, desperately.

When the ball dropped, Bertie Auld, the cool, composed veteran, was waiting for it and he got to it first and he lashed it into the net. Then he was holding his hands high in exultation and poor Saints, bewildered Saints, who could themselves have been in the lead, were a goal down in two minutes.

The neutrals felt sorry for St. Johnstone. In spite of their match words of confidence, they were panicky, all at sea in Hampden. Celtic were moving with skill and fire and confidence.

Hood hammered a Craig cut-back over the bar. A Craig header whistled inches wide. Hughes caused consternation every time he had the ball. Once he missed an open goal from four yards. McNeill headed too high. Chalmers shot recklessly and when Donaldson had been tempted outside his penalty area Hughes shot past.

St. Johnstone had their moments at Hampden and John Fallon, one of the Celtic heroes, makes a superb save from Benny Rooney in the closing seconds to save his side

Celtic were rampant and these chances were devised from swift interlocking football, with Auld in the middle using the ball with accuracy and cunning. And Bobby Murdoch was superb, backing all the moves with power and intelligence.

Fifteen minutes had gone before St. Johnstone settled to any sort of game and they were lucky not to be at least five goals down by then.

Here it was, however, that Saints gained admiration—for their pluck, for their skill, for their fight-back. Their training, their practice had not been in vain.

GREAT TROUBLE

The massacre of Saints didn't happen. For 20 minutes Celtic had been incredibly brilliant, threatening to collect an astonishing total of goals. Then Saints stepped in and settled to make an excellent contest, with the speed and style of Connolly and Hall in the middle of the attack causing McNeill and Brogan great trouble.

The Celtic skipper was happy to head over his own bar when under pressure and then Brogan brought Connolly down on the penalty line, with all Perth swearing it was inside.

Saints, though, had an undeserved stroke of ill-luck in the 35th minute. McCarry, who wore a No. 9 but worked prodigiously in mid-field, damaged a knee and had to be taken off. Whitelaw came on in his place.

And Saints' luck was still right out when McNeill made a tremendous clearance, coming from nowhere to divert a swift Hall shot that seemed net-bound.

The second half was a classic. Steve Chalmers was injured in the 50th minute and, to a roar of acclaim from his admirers, Jimmy Johnstone came on.

St. Johnstone fought back and it became a magnificent final, one of the greatest. It was fast and thrilling with attacks sprung by great passes.

The pace never let up.

Fallon made a brilliant save from Whitelaw. Gordon stopped Hughes superbly when the big centre-forward was through. Hood flicked a Callaghan corner over the bar. Fallon made a double-barrelled save from Hall. Johnstone was through but paused too long.

The final minutes were furious and memorable. Donaldson passed out to Coburn. The back turned and Hughes jumped in, robbed the goalkeeper, who had been given the ball nearly back, and shot into the net. It looked a goal but the referee awarded a free-kick against Hughes.

Then goalkeeper Donaldson had his name taken after challenging Hood.

But it was Celtic 'keeper John Fallon who was the real hero. With seconds to go, a curling Aird shot was pushed round the post by the diving 'keeper. Then Rooney cracked the ball with all his might—and clutched his head in despair and astonishment as Fallon turned the ball round the other post.

GALLANT LOSERS

That was the end. Saints had lost. But they took great credit as the most gallant losers Hampden has ever seen.

St. Johnstone's tragedy was that they left it too late before turning on their real style.

They had proved, however, that, despite dull days to come as reaction to the defeat set in, they had the will and the skill and the managerial know-how to become one of Scotland's finest teams.

St. Johnstone goalkeeper Donaldson in hetic action in the League Cup Final

The life and hard times of the goalkeeper...

WHY is this man looking so thoughtful? Because he is a goalkeeper, that's why. He is Gerry Neef, of Rangers. And, like all goalkeepers, he is perhaps wondering if it's all worthwhile.

For the life and hard times of goalkeepers are hardly calculated to bring eternal smiles to the faces of the men who guard the nets.

It's true they are sometimes heroes. It's true they can be cheered to the echo for magnificent saves.

But at other times...Oh, brother...They are the lads who usually get the blame for losing a goal. They are howled at by their colleagues. They are jeered by the fans. They are criticised for making easy saves look difficult, for being too acrobatic, too rash, for having butter fingers, for failing to leave their goal, for sticking in their goal, for punching instead of clutching, for clutching instead of punching, for throwing the ball instead of kicking it, for taking up the wrong position.

As a great goalie once said: 'You don't have to be daft to be a goalkeeper—but it certainly helps.'

And yet...keepers love their job. Even if they're laughed at for making unorthodox saves. Even if their goal can be a hell-box. Even if they're threatened and harassed by attackers.

For the keepers feel there is no business like goal business.

And now—presenting high drama, fun and fury from the life and hectic affairs of some Scottish goalkeepers...

JOHNNY-ON-THE-SPOT

That's flying Ian Dick, of Partick
Thistle, who dives in at just the
right time to save in a game
against Rangers

TWO'S A CROWD

And sometimes it gets pretty crowded in the goalmouth (left). David Stewart, of Ayr United, doesn't mind a visit of this kind, though. The Rangers ball landed on the roof of the net

DID IT HURT?

Well, that's one way of saving it. Or—how Gordon Marshall got his nose in front. It may have been painful; nevertheless, the gallant Hibernian goalkeeper stopped the shot from Willie Wallace in a game against Celtic

FULL STRETCH

It's not all quiet on the keeping front—and here is Ayr's Stewart (above) seen making a fine save from a Colin Stein shot. Frustration for Rangers

TRAGIC STORY

No words are needed to express the disgust of Airdrie's Roddie McKenzie after the ball flies into his net

ALL IN VAIN

A great leap—but it's in vain. For a great enemy of Scottish goalkeepers has struck—Tommy Gemmell, Celtic back with the dynamic shot. Willie Duff, Dunfermline's keeper, hadn't a chance with this fierce drive from Gemmell

LOOK! NO HEAD

Down—but anything but out. Aberdeen's Ernie McGarr saves in unorthodox but effective style in a fierce Dunfermline raid

FRIENDS?

Who said the keeper was the loneliest man in football? Not David Stewart, of Ayr United, who finds himself with company as a huge crowd surges into Somerset Park for the visit of Rangers

LOOK AT THAT

Aye, aye, just watch it...it wasn't my fault...it was yours. That's what Morton's Scandinavian keeper Lief Nielsen (right) seems to be saying after the ball lands in his net during a match with Rangers

WRONG WAY

Ach, that's goal business. That must have been the rueful thought of St. Mirren's Jim Thorburn as he goes the wrong way to a penalty scored by Davie Provan, of Rangers

YOUNG STAR

But tragedy is far from the thoughts of this young man who looks like Cliff Richard. He is Alex Morrison, of Hamilton Acas. Alex is only 15, the youngest keeper in Scotland—but he's starry-eyed—and thinks keeping goal is the greatest job in the world.

Nightmare
in Lisbon

For everyone in the merry party, it seemed too good to be true.

Back home in Scotland snow covered the land for it was bleak November. But here in Portugal the sun shone brightly.

For Celtic and the sports reporters who accompanied them, magic was everywhere. In the warm air, in the scent of flowers that still bloomed under the gently waving palms. In the luxurious atmosphere of the Hotel Palacio, where the club had stayed when they won the European Cup on that never-to-be forgotten May night of 1967.

Spirits couldn't have been higher. A smooth jet had whisked us in under three hours from chilly Scotland to the warmly glowing millionaire's paradise that is Estoril. Celtic were back to the scene of their headiest triumph—and everything was going their way.

Celtic were in the European Cup again and playing in a country which would for ever live in their memories. This time they were not bound for the exotic, tree-fringed amphitheatre of Portugal's National Stadium, where they had been crowned kings of Europe. This time the Portuguese would not be joyously supporting them, as they had when Inter-Milan, arch-priests of defensive soccer, were their opponents in the final. This time they faced the heroes of Portugal.

Still, Celtic felt things just could not go wrong. After all, they were three goals up from the first leg of the European Cup second-round tie with Benfica, the eagles of Lisbon, and the fans of the Portuguese champions looked glum and assured the Scots the tie was as good as won.

So there was little of the tension which usually envelopes a team abroad on European Cup business.

We of the Press enjoyed it, too. For once, the telephone calls came in on time on clear lines. And we could relax for an hour or two on Estoril's golf course, take a dip in the hotel pool, toy with a lobster thermidor in Cascais's Pescador restaurant and wash down the succulent morsels with deep draughts of vino vherde.

For once, too, I could agree with envious friends who keep telling me it must be marvellous to travel all over the world with football teams.

There was hardly a cloud in the blue sky. Celtic trained happily, conscientiously, and we paid a sentimental return visit to the nearby National Stadium.

It was just too good to be true.

And it was.

My first premonition of personal disaster came as soon as we arrived at the imposing Estadio da Luz, the stadium of light, where the second leg between Benfica and Celtic was to be played in Lisbon on the night of 26 November 1969.

Not for a moment, even then, however, did I think Celtic would be in trouble. My thoughts were selfish. I was concerned about my telephone.

As always, the kick-off in Portugal was late, timed for 10.45 p.m. And that doesn't give a reporter for a daily newspaper much margin for error. We would miss our first edition, anyhow. But would I be in time for any edition? My head was full of foreboding and I recalled gloomily our dreadful

A great Celtic, Steve Chalmers.
His thrust was missed in Lisbon.
Chalmers was injured earlier in
the season

experiences at the European Cup Final in 1967 when many of us were on the line for almost five hours, unable to hear anyone at the Scottish end.

And this time facilities looked worse than they had been in the National Stadium. Benfica's ground is marvellous, a spectacular, towering stadium, dramatic in the brilliant floodlighting, with the club's symbols, the eagles, shining metallically from their eyries above the pylons.

But the visiting journalists were packed into a box which was more like a pigeon loft than an eagle's roomy abode and we were seated, jostling shoulders and arms, as uncomfortably as sardines.

That didn't worry me as much, though, as the sight of the telephones, hand-sets which seemed to have been snatched from an antique dealer. I shuddered and I remembered hours of waiting for calls in Budapest, Belgrade, Tiflis, Kiev, Katovice, Nojvodina and Mexico City, remembered lines which went dead or clicked, clacked and buzzed so noisily that speech was impossible. No wonder my hands were shaking when, miraculously, my phone tinkled five minutes before the kick-off and Glasgow was on the line.

I almost cheered with relief. And it was as well I didn't. For no sooner had I dictated the teams to my office in Glasgow than . . . screech, gabble, squawk, gibberish . . . and the line went dead.

For nearly an hour my Portuguese paradise turned into a hell as I tried vainly to get through. I tried to concentrate on what was happening on the field, to take a few notes, as I shouted and howled and tried all the tricks I have learned in countless expeditions abroad to get re-connected.

If my world had collapsed, however, so had Celtic's. They had started, coolly, calmly, almost cheekily. Their aim was to hold Benfica, a dispirited Benfica who had

a half-fit Eusebio out in a bid to snatch an early goal but who were without their great tall centre-forward Torres, who had been injured. Celtic played a 4–3–3 and it seemed to be working perfectly, with Jimmy Johnstone enjoying himself with brilliant bursts.

Then, just when it seemed they had succeeded in their aim of taking all the starch out of Benfica, Celtic became too cocky. In 36 minutes, a moment of hesitation allowed Eusebio to head a great goal. Three minutes later Graca scored a second. The Benfica fans were chanting their delight. Celtic were in dire trouble.

And still there was silence on my phone and I couldn't get one word over to Glasgow.

I was hoarse with screaming, my hands shaking with anxiety, my brow dripping sweat.

Now the game was really ablaze. Suddenly Benfica players lost their heads.

Bertie Auld was butted. Then Jimmy Johnstone was laid low in another savage attack. For a moment it seemed that all hell was about to break loose. But the Celtic players, to their eternal credit, kept their heads and refused to retaliate. That was hard to do but the Celts had learned the facts of football life in the torrid cauldrons of South America as well as Europe and knew it was fatal to lift a fist, to hit back in any way. For in modern football the way of the retaliator brings greater punishment than it does to the transgressor who fouls first.

They were rightly bitter, however, when Dutch referee Van Raavens did not even caution the Benfica strongarm men for attacks which ruined their reputation for sporting play.

At half-time the match which was to have been a placid exercise for Celtic had turned into a cliff-hanger, with the Scottish

Tommy Gemmell . . . he scored a fine goal in the first leg with Benfica

champions on the ropes, worried, their confidence shattered.

Disaster stared the Celts in the face.

It had already overwhelmed me.

Not one word of the sensational game had gone back to the *Daily Record* in Glasgow.

The line was still dead.

'Meester, meester.' There was a tap on my shoulder and I looked into a smiling Portuguese face. 'Go away,' I snapped. I was in no mood to tell a Lisbon journalist what I thought about the game. But he wasn't a journalist. He was a telephone engineer.

'You 'ave trouble, no?' he asked. But he didn't wait for my reply, which couldn't be printed here, anyhow. He seemed to know what was wrong and quickly started to install a new telephone set on the desk.

The minutes were long as he fiddled with wires and connections and put in new batteries in the primitive container below the desk. But he knew what he was doing. At last, he stood up, bowed and said: 'You try now.'

And it was a miracle. At last the telephone worked. I thanked him and in a few minutes I was through to my office in Glasgow, dictating a quick summary of the exciting first half, then taking up the thread in running commentary of the second session.

THE GAME GOES ON

At last, all was going well. Celtic had settled. Benfica were without Eusebio, who hadn't returned after the interval. The crowd lost much of their enthusiasm as they saw Benfica's chances fading.

My line to Glasgow was faint but I knew my copy was going over.

As the game drew to a close, however, the tension became unbearable. Benfica mounted last-gasp attacks. They threw everything into their raids. But now it was difficult for the reporters to see what was going on. Right in front of us excitable Benfica fans were standing up on their seats, howling on their side.

HIGH TENSION

What I could see, though, was the big clock behind the Celtic goal. And the hand of the clock had long ago passed the finishing mark.

Would the game never end? In the first half, the clock had broken down but the session had ended right on the stroke of the 45th minute. What was going on now?

Three minutes extra-time had been played. Still Celtic were holding out. Still Benfica attacked. At last referee Van Raavens looked at his linesmen, waved his hands in a gesture which seemed to announce the match was over and Celtic were through by 3–2.

But the game still went on.

Celtic fans were biting their nails. I was shouting into my phone, counting off the seconds, saying, 'The game is now 3 minutes 20 seconds of overtime. . . ."

And Benfica were given a free-kick on the edge of the penalty box. Again the referee looked at a linesman—and waved his hands. But the free-kick was taken and the ball flashed over the Celtic goal and there was a moment of indecision among the defenders and there was Diamantino, who had come on as a substitute, on the spot to head the ball into the net.

Confusion reigned. Hundreds of overjoyed Benfica fans poured on to the field. Was it a goal? No one knew. At first I thought the referee had blown for time before the ball went into the net. As soon as police had made a way for the players among the milling fans on the pitch the referee led them off the field. The ball was not re-centred.

Then came the news that the goal counted, that the players would come back out in five minutes to play 30 minutes extra time.

Now it was getting on for midnight. I had almost lost my voice—but the show had to go on. 'Just carry on with a comment of run of play in the extra time,' I was told. As time was running out for my newspaper's editions, I didn't have to turn in a complete re-write of the game, a critical analysis, which is our usual practice. A short introduction would do, to be followed by the run of play copy I had already sent. 'O.K.,' I said—and sat back to describe the vital 30 minutes of extra time.

I didn't sit back for long. In exactly three minutes, my phone went dead again. This time, so did all the others. A Lisbon official, believing the game was over, had pulled out the plug which connected all the special lines to Britain for the game—and gone home.

If there was tension on the field, it was nothing to the consternation in that little Press-box which, despite the cool of the night, had become a black hole of Lisbon.

The game went on, with narrow escapes at both ends. As it ended, with neither side adding to the score, which was 3–3 on aggregate, lethargy had set in among the harassed reporters. For there was just nothing we could do, except wait until someone in authority connected us again to our home bases.

Just behind us, however, in the referee's room, another drama was beginning. A toss of a silver Dutch 2½-guilder piece would decide whether Benfica or Celtic would go through to the next round of the European Cup.

It was a dreadful way to decide an important tie but it was the rule.

In the Press box we were just as anxious as the Celtic fans who crowded round outside. Suddenly a great cheer went up and again the Benfica fans, gay in red favours, danced and sang on the field.

But it was only a rumour. A minute later a colleague who had seen the drama in the referee's room burst into the Press box to announce that Celtic captain Billy McNeill had called 'Heads'—and won the toss.

Celtic were through. And around 1.30 in the morning I was through, too, to my office. I had managed to get in touch with a Lisbon telephone operator, who had taken pity on me and given me a line to Glasgow.

It was over. Celtic had won. The *Daily Record* had the story.

And, at 3 a.m., my arm still stiff from holding that confounded phone, my throat parched and my hearing almost nil, I had the most welcome drink I've enjoyed in my life.

I only wish I could have seen that Portuguese telephone engineer to have given him one, too.

If it hadn't been for him, I would now be writing the saddest Lisbon story ever. . .